ALLEN COUNTY PUBLIC LIBRARY

3 1833 01566 9234

Y0-BSM-443

128.2 M66   FEB 2 5 1992

THE MIND AND BEYOND

DO NOT REMOVE
CARDS FROM POCKET

ALLEN COUNTY PUBLIC LIBRARY

FORT WAYNE, INDIANA 46802

You may return this book to any agency, branch,
or bookmobile of the Allen County Public Library.

DEMCO

The Mind and Beyond

The Mind and Beyond

Allen County Public Library
Ft. Wayne, Indiana

CONTENTS

Where Monsters Lurk amid Heaven's Secrets

Is it a ghost they are chasing?" asks a neuroscientist as he reflects on the continuing and frustrating quest for understanding of the human mind. "Or something concrete and measurable?" Such questions come more easily than answers: How does the physical brain relate to thought and consciousness? Does the self—an individual's mental being—reside in some secure corner of that organ? Or is each of us a mere flurry of electrochemical activity flickering across the spaces between minuscule cells, vulnerable as an unstored computer message in a thunderstorm? After centuries of increasingly scientific study, the human brain—and the mind, if that is a separate entity—remains among the most enigmatic phenomena in the cosmos.

Even theories of the brain that have wide scientific support trail clouds of mystery in their wakes. Deep within the roughly three-pound mass of pinkish gray matter, for instance, far below the more recently evolved outer surface where activities like logic and language formation are believed to occur, squats an old brain section called the cerebellum. The cerebellum coordinates the body's muscles. Some believe it is also home to terrifying ancient creature images that refuse to be

banished from human awareness—werewolves, vampires, demons—and, moreover, may be the source of paranormal experiences, such as the spirit voices that speak through entranced mediums.

Among the mind's amazing riddles are uncanny abilities sometimes linked to disabling brain disorders. Victims of a strange syndrome called synesthesia, for example, receive messages from their senses through a brain switchboard gone haywire; they may taste colors, feel flavors, and see sounds. Some can read while blindfolded, by passing their fingertips over the page. And people known as savants may have the intelligence of preschoolers yet be able to memorize an entire telephone book in a single reading. Many of them reportedly possess a capacity for extrasensory perception as well.

But the most intriguing puzzle is also the most basic—the very nature of the mind itself. Like many other philosophers of the past, sixteenth-century Italian cosmologist Giordano Bruno believed the human mind was divine and contained all the secrets of heaven. In the Western world, science eroded that view over the centuries until the very opposite was generally held true: The mind could be nothing more nor less than the sum total of the physical brain's activity. Recent decades have witnessed a profound and surprising shift in this attitude among many thinkers, some of them scientists, as the accounts that launch this exploration of the mind's marvels and mysteries will show.

CHAPTER 1

The Cosmos Within

ne day in 1973, an elderly gentleman marched up a hill behind his farmhouse outside Montreal carrying a basketful of old cans of house paint. When he reached a large boulder on the slope of the hill, he took brush in hand and began painting a series of images on the surface of the rock. First he wrote *pneuma,* the Greek word for "spirit"; next he painted a torch, representing the enterprise of science; then, on the other side of the rock, he drew a human head, a brain within it, and at the brain's center, a question mark. Finally, he connected all the images with a solid line.

The man was eighty-two-year-old Wilder Penfield, an eminent Canadian neurosurgeon, then retired and writing what would prove to be his last book, *The Mystery of the Mind.* The work dealt with the relationship of mind, brain, and science, and the strange hieroglyphs he had painted on the rock expressed Penfield's conviction that in time scientific study of the brain would illuminate all the secrets of the mind.

During his long career as a skilled brain surgeon and astute observer, Penfield had added significantly to scientific understanding of how the body's most complex organ works. He had developed several neurosurgical treatments for brain injuries, particularly for epilepsy. At the end of his career, he was convinced that all the varied responses of the human mind—the feelings, desires, thoughts, dreams, and perceptions that together make up consciousness—were caused by chemical and electrical interactions among the brain's billions of tiny nerve cells. Thus the capabilities of the mind, Penfield held, were determined wholly by the physical activity within the grapefruit-size lump of pinkish gray matter encased by the skull.

Yet, a year and a half after his first painting safari—and a mere six months before he died—Penfield made another trip up the hill carrying paint bucket and brush. Swaddled in sweaters to protect against the frigid winter winds, he revised his artwork. When he had finished, the painting illustrated a very different principle from that of the original: Where there had been a solid line of confidence joining the images on both sides of the rock, there was now a broken line of uncertainty. At age eighty-four, after half a century spent shoring up the prevailing scientific position, Penfield had had a change of heart. It is highly improbable, he admitted with that dashed line, that a strictly physical approach will ever yield a full explanation of consciousness. The mind, Penfield was saying, is far more than a by-product of the material brain's ability to process information.

Penfield's apostasy graphically illustrates a major breach that has divided the multitudes of scientists, philosophers, and theologians who through the centuries have delved into the nature of the human mind. Roughly speaking, a battle line has been drawn between two camps: On one side are the so-called materialists, who believe that mental processes—thoughts, feelings, the ability to reason—are merely a result of neurons firing within the brain. On the other side are the dualists, who hold that the body is a physical entity and the mind a spiritual one; each exists separately, they believe, with little or no interaction or influence on one another.

For almost three centuries, since Isaac Newton proposed his elegant clockwork universe, the austere scientific tenets of the materialists have governed Western exploration of the brain and consciousness. Mystical and spiritual approaches to an understanding of the mind have largely been dismissed as fancies lying outside the strict boundaries of scientific inquiry. Yet that same span of time has seen a number of scholars and scientists, among them Wilder Penfield, defect from the classical camp. More and more, these learned men and women have begun to suspect that the many-splendored

realm of consciousness cannot be explained solely by physical phenomena. As Penfield himself put it shortly before he died, "the consciousness of man, the mind, is something not to be reduced to brain mechanisms."

In the field of neuroscience, studies of human brains damaged by birth defects, accident, illness, or surgery have revealed that these afflicted people sometimes exhibit perplexing mental and perceptual capabilities that seem to some brain researchers to emanate from a "second self" or inner spirit. These observers believe they have glimpsed signs of a higher will that appears to draw its power not from the physical being but from some nonmaterial source beyond the reach of scientific instruments. In exploring altered states of consciousness induced variously by dreams, meditative trances, and drugs, they claim to have found hints of a larger, unseen spiritual reality underlying the physical world; an attunement to this invisible realm, they speculate, may account for such psychic phenomena as precognition, psychokinesis, and a sense of enlightenment or oneness with the universe.

Even more surprising, support for this shift in thinking about the mind has come from the "hardest" science of all, physics. Ephemeral puzzles about the nature of consciousness are not normal concerns for physicists, but as they have probed deeper into the strange environs of the subatomic world, these scientists have discovered that within the atom, the orderly rules of behavior governing larger objects such as baseballs and

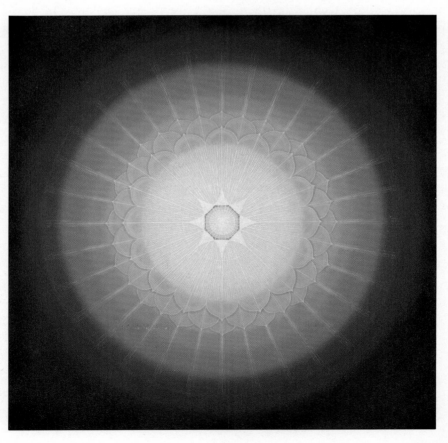

planets no longer apply. Here, matter and energy become all but indistinguishable, and the predictability of the Newtonian universe gives way to probability, to the iffiness of dice games and weather forecasting.

From the quantum perspective, the universe is not only a collection of mechanical components, like a Tinkertoy, but is also an indivisible whole, and all its parts, including the human mind, act on and are acted on by every other part. Some well-respected physicists have gone so far as to contend that without the perceiving mind of human beings, the universe as we know it would not exist at all—the mind, they say, may be the lens that focuses a world of random events into the ordered reality we perceive.

Speculations like this uncannily echo the ancient teachings of Eastern mystics, who professed the interconnectedness of consciousness and cosmos centuries before the emergence of scientific inquiry. Occasionally employing logic but more frequently relying on intuition, the founders and practitioners of such Eastern religions and philosophies as Hinduism, Buddhism, and Taoism conceived holistic portraits of the universe in which mind and matter merge and flow seamlessly one into the other. For example, more than 1,500 years before quantum physics was developed, a basic text of Buddhism called the *Avatamsaka Sutra* taught that consciousness and the material world, which to the unenlightened mind appear irrevocably divided from one another, are in fact joined in a smooth continuity known in Sanskrit as the *dharmakaya,* or "body of the great order."

As awareness of these converging world views has grown in the West, the study of consciousness, its origins and operations, has emerged as one of the most important intellectual pursuits of the late twentieth century. To many anxious observers, Western culture seems bent on a disastrous course of ecological exploitation and unbridled acquisitiveness, and some philosophers are suggesting that only a totally new approach to the understanding of consciousness—what Kenneth Pelletier, a popular author on the subject, describes as "a new science of conscious-

ness"—will set society on a straighter path. Pelletier predicts that the order of thought that favors the material over the spiritual and separates the ephemeral mind from the physical brain will give way to a new, holistic order, which melds the two seemingly contradictory strains.

The debate over the origins of consciousness has been raging since at least the time of Plato. The Greek philosopher was among the first to argue that the human mind was an entity unto itself, existing independently of the body. And although anatomically he placed the mind within the brain, he denied any intercourse between the two. The brain, Plato believed, was a sphere—the perfect geometric shape, according to ancient Greeks—and thus a fitting repository for what he considered the essence of humanity.

During the Middle Ages, Christian philosophers developed their own theory about the seat of consciousness, one that perpetuated the dualistic mind-body split: God was the source of all thoughts and feelings, and these emanated from a point just a few inches above the head. Beginning about the fifteenth century, the natural sciences began to challenge the Church's view of the universe. But it was in the hands of seventeenth-century French mathematician and philosopher René Descartes that echoes of Platonic dualism, the Church's sacred order, and the prevailing logic of the day would mutate and merge to form the school of thought known as Cartesian dualism.

From the age of twenty-three, René Descartes's ambition was to develop a universal, scientific method of reasoning; one which, when applied to any type of data, would offer up conclusions that would be readily verifiable. Only when the results in every science were as certain as those achieved in mathematics, he believed, would the claim to have obtained knowledge be justified. By applying the disciplines of science, with its rigorous pursuit of empirical proof, to matters of philosophy, Descartes effectively devised the ground rules by which Western science would abide for centuries to come.

Descartes earned his commanding influence by the

Philosopher René Descartes is captured at his work in this late-1700s portrait. The Frenchman was a devout Catholic and rooted his writings on the human mind and other topics in firm convictions about the beneficence of God and the immortality of the soul. Nonetheless, Church officials banned his books in 1663, finding blasphemy in his assertion that the body was like a machine.

brilliant range and sheer volume of his scholarly output. In addition to defining the guiding principles of the emerging scientific outlook, he advanced the practice of analytic geometry, teased out the laws of mathematical physics, and explored a diverse number of philosophical issues from the essence of the soul to the nature of freedom.

Such ruminations eventually led him to divide the world's myriad aspects into two basic categories, or "simple natures": the physical, which included all physical properties and actions; and the mental, which encompassed all thoughts, feelings, and desires. Descartes discerned that human beings combined the two natures, but he decreed that the physical and mental arenas were essentially distinct—that is, neither had more than a limited effect on the other. Of the two, the philosopher considered the realm of

thought the most exalted: It belonged distinctively to humans. In fact, asserted Descartes, thought was the singular trademark of the human soul, "which needs no space to exist in, and does not depend on any material thing" for its vigor. In his scheme, the thinking mind was a gift from God and issued from the spiritual plane. Like Plato before him, Descartes lent anatomical credibility to his theory by locating the seat of the "rational soul," or mind, in the brain. He even went so far as to pinpoint a spot at the top of the brain called the pineal gland.

This tiny, tear-shaped body, which is believed to play a significant role in sexual maturation and in adaptation to changes in seasons and light, is also known as the third eye, and it was believed by some ancient cultures to have mystical powers. Descartes, though, decided that the role of

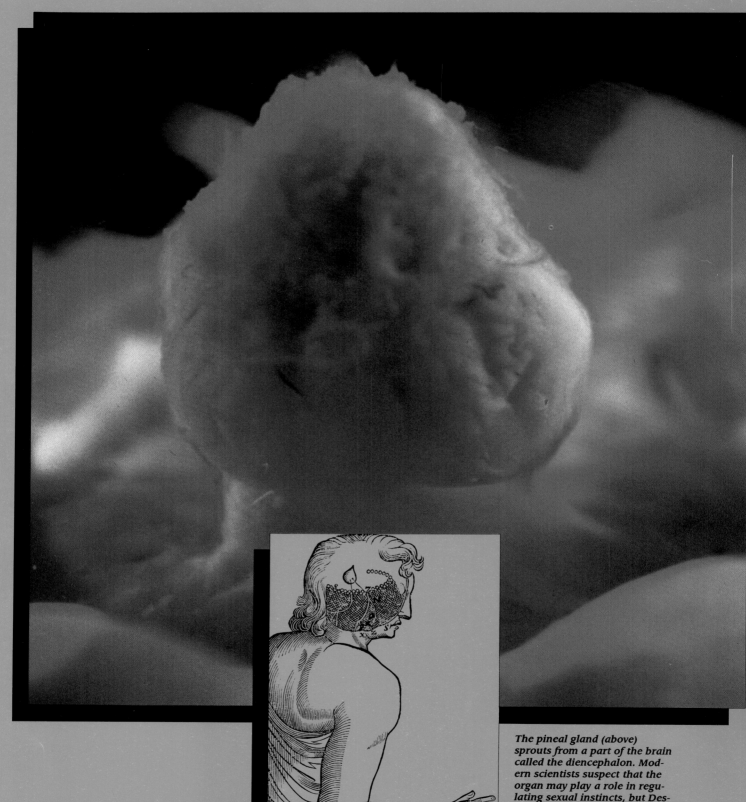

The pineal gland (above) sprouts from a part of the brain called the diencephalon. Modern scientists suspect that the organ may play a role in regulating sexual instincts, but Descartes thought it served a broader purpose in mediating between the body and the mind. In the diagram at left, he sought to show how the pineal gland might alert the nervous system to the sensation of heat.

the pineal gland was to act as a point of contact for the body and the mind. By way of the gland, he speculated, the mind propels a bloodlike fluid called animal spirits through the body to stimulate movement in the nerves and muscles. Conversely, changes in the body as perceived by the sense organs are transmitted by the same animal spirits to the pineal gland; there the fluids deliver their sensory messages to the mind. What a person perceives, then, according to Descartes, is not the sight of an actual chair or the breeze-ruffled curtains at an open window but instead the flow of the spirits within the brain produced by the eyes' signals.

Thus reality was only indirectly perceived. Descartes could never be sure what the reality of "chair" or "curtains" was, but he knew without doubt that he was *thinking* about them. Thought was the only thing he was sure of—hence his famous dictum, "I think, therefore I am."

In venerating consciousness as a manifestation of God's work, Descartes's dualistic approach seemed to put further study of the mind outside the scientist's venue. God took care of mental (that is, spiritual) matters; a scientist's proper concern was confined to physical things that could be measured, weighed, and tested. Yet it was Descartes's great insights on the logic of scientific discourse, among other factors, that led later scientists to denounce his insistence on a separation of mental and physical activity. For eighteenth-century critics of Cartesian dualism such as French physician and philosopher Julien Offroy de La Mettrie or English philosopher Thomas Hobbes, the only supportable position for a thinking person on the mind-body problem was materialistic monism—the theory that all things in nature, from waves on the shore to a person's memories or desires, were material in essence and could ultimately be unraveled with reference to physical laws.

Hobbes contended that humans were automatons, driven by the stirrings of atoms in their brains much as machines are driven by springs and wheels. La Mettrie was particularly impressed by the engineering attainments of the day—among his favorite technological achievements was a celebrated mechanical duck that could paddle and "digest" food—and he contended in a 1748 essay that the soul was merely "an enlightened machine."

Common sense seems to argue that feelings, such as anger or love, have an influence on physical behavior. But strict materialists like Hobbes and La Mettrie found it inconceivable that a subjective mood could possibly have an effect on the functioning cells of the brain. They were convinced that the insubstantial web of mental activity could be the result only of physical processes, and was not a ghostly manifestation of the divine. They began to advance a dominant materialistic argument: If science could fully map the structure of the brain and monitor the coursing of the blood and communication of the nerves, all the mind's activities would be shown to be by-products of material interactions.

In the context of the nineteenth-century Victorian Age, which was inclined to celebrate all things mechanical, materialism attained the status of dogma, and a wave of interest in the natural sciences swept through intellectual circles and popular culture alike. After Charles Darwin and Alfred Russel Wallace elucidated the theory of natural selection in 1858, natural historians strove to trace the origin of consciousness in the starkly mechanistic perspective of evolution. Scientists became obsessed with the goal of determining how, when, and why consciousness had evolved.

Certainly not all scientists embraced Darwin's theories about evolution, but those who did reasoned that the emergence of a sophisticated consciousness must have provided humans with an adaptive advantage, or else it would not have become part of our standard equipment. Like the ability to swim or to fly, the ability to think—and to be aware of the process—had to have conveyed a benefit to humans that made it more likely that the offspring of parents possessing the trait would thrive over those who lacked it. Theories abounded. Perhaps consciousness enabled human beings to work together more efficiently, so they could better carry out the tasks of feeding and defending themselves. Or maybe consciousness served to aid them in predicting the outcome of actions in an environment ever bristling with threats, thus increasing the odds of avoiding injury or death.

As these evolutionary speculations were bandied about in the period leading up to and following the turn of the century, students of consciousness were confronted by a basic question: What is consciousness, and do only humans have it? The American psychologist and philosopher William James defined consciousness as "the pursuance of future ends and the choice of means for their attainment." By this measure, James found that even a headless frog could be said to have consciousness.

Experiments conducted on a frog whose head had been surgically removed had shown that if one of the frog's legs were bound in place and electrically stimulated, another leg would reach up to bat away the source of the irritation. To James, this was clearly a purposeful gesture and indicated that, by his definition at least, the frog was conscious. Carrying out systematic observations of the animal world, other investigators detected similarly complex behaviors in a wide range of creatures from amoebas to wasps to baboons.

The notion that "lower orders" of creatures might be able to think upset Victorian sensibilities. Instead of confronting the biases of the era, some Victorian scientists deemphasized the importance of consciousness in general, even for humans. Theorists such as Shadworth Hodgson and Thomas Henry Huxley, both British, argued that mental awareness was like a decoration on a building: It added interest but served no real purpose. Hodgson used another analogy in writing about feelings, saying they were "mere colors laid on the surface of a mosaic which is held together by its stones and not by the colors." Huxley, in 1896, called human beings "conscious automata," implying that the mind had no influence on humankind's activities or evolution. Today, Princeton psychologist Julian Jaynes describes this concept as the "helpless spectator" theory of consciousness. By this way of thinking, according to Jaynes, "consciousness can no more modify the working mechanism of the body or its behavior than can the whistle of a train modify its machinery or where it goes. Moan as it will, the tracks have long ago decided where the train will go."

Here and there, a few voices were raised from within the scientific establishment in dissent from this uncompromising materialism. One was that of Alfred Russel Wallace, codiscoverer with Darwin of the principles of natural selection and evolution. Born in 1823, Wallace worked as a schoolmaster, surveyor, and architect before developing an interest in botany. He became an ardent naturalist who undertook expeditions in the Amazon River basin and in the Malay Archipelago to collect insects. It was during such an expedition in 1858, Wallace later wrote, that, while in the throes of a fever, "There suddenly flashed upon me the idea of the survival of the fittest." Although Wallace was entirely unaware of it, this was essentially the same idea that had struck Darwin almost twenty years earlier.

In 1870, Wallace published *Contributions to the Theory of Natural Selection,* in which he described the ways that natural selection worked to provide through evolution certain physical features that benefited some creatures over others, such as the markings of their coats or the shape of their limbs. These principles applied to humans as well, of course, but when it came to the human mind, Wallace had a problem. He found himself unable to understand how the same physical processes could have yielded the self-awareness of human beings. Wallace's education and experience had disposed him to fit consciousness into a materialistic framework, but the longer he pondered the facts, the less convinced he became that mental states could be attributed solely to physical evolutionary forces.

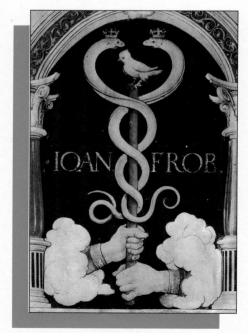

In the caduceus, the emblem of the medical profession, the dove perched atop the snake-entwined staff has been interpreted as a symbol of the pineal gland poised over the spinal cord.

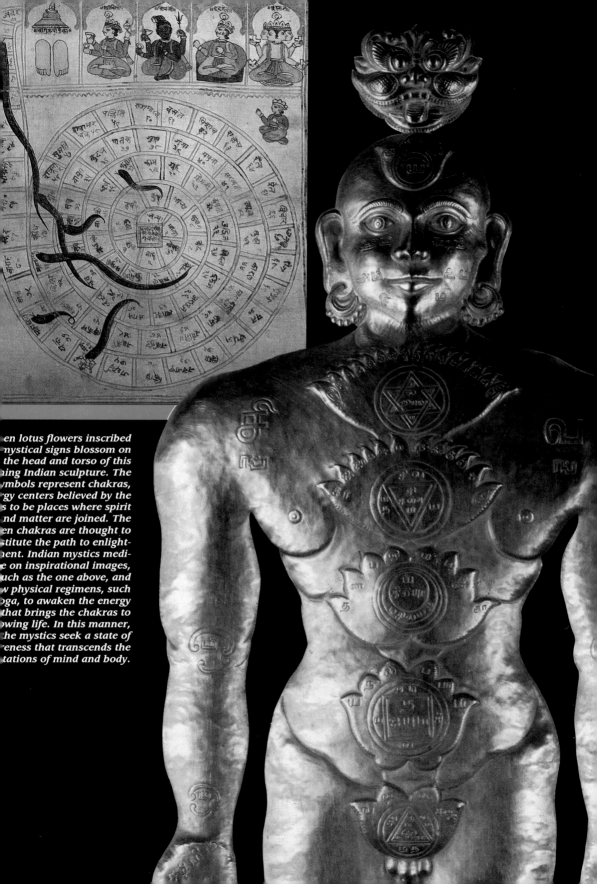

...en lotus flowers inscribed ...mystical signs blossom on ...the head and torso of this ...ing Indian sculpture. The ...ymbols represent chakras, ...gy centers believed by the ...s to be places where spirit ...nd matter are joined. The ...en chakras are thought to ...stitute the path to enlight-...ent. Indian mystics medi-...e on inspirational images, ...uch as the one above, and ...w physical regimens, such ...oga, to awaken the energy ...that brings the chakras to ...owing life. In this manner, ...he mystics seek a state of ...reness that transcends the ...tations of mind and body.

Caluaria auulſa de arbore pendet.
Duram matrem oſtendit, per quã ita deerrant
venæ ſurſum à iugularibus internis vtrin-
que delatæ, quemadmodum ſupra dictum
eſt. Cuius medium ita finditur vt vides, &
ligamentoſum eſt admodum.

Having deposited his pate on a tree limb, a man leans forward to display his brain in this sixteenth-century woodcut. The Latin inscription likens the pattern of the brain's fissures to the form of a tree. Such a comparison was typical of the scientific view known as monism, which sought to demystify nature by showing that all life processes, even mental ones, conformed to physical laws.

Several years before publishing his book on natural selection, Wallace had begun to attend spiritualist gatherings in England that were directed by well-known mediums of the day. At first, Wallace had no use for spiritual phenomena. But on a number of occasions he witnessed things that he, and many others, believed could not be scientifically explained. Victorian séances, for instance, produced startling displays: spirit rapping, in which sharp knocking sounds issued from tables without evident cause; levitation of people into the air by no visible means; and direct or automatic writing, in which messages appeared, seemingly spontaneously, on pieces of paper. Observing these alleged marvels, Wallace became fascinated by psychic phenomena, which he eventually concluded "are proved, quite as well as any facts are proved in other sciences."

From here it was a short step for Wallace to become convinced that the human mind "could not possibly have been developed by means of the same laws which have determined the progressive development of the organic world in general and also of man's physical organism." Instead, Wallace said, a metaphysical intervention must have taken place at two specific points in the course of human evolution to create consciousness: first to strike the initial spark of awareness in the humanoid brain and then again to spur the emergence of the first true civilizations.

Wallace pursued his investigations into the occult until his death in 1913. Although he was honored by the Order of Merit for his scientific researches in 1910, it is likely that his fame as a developer of the evolution theory was eroded in part by the derision some of his scientific peers heaped on his spiritualistic beliefs. Science, they declared, had no room for occult nonsense. Besides, for many scientists Wallace's misgivings about the evolution of consciousness had been rendered moot by a new point of view that emerged around the turn of the century.

By then, some brain researchers were proudly claiming to have solved the thorny issue bequeathed them by Huxley—that is, why consciousness should have evolved if it served no adaptive purpose. They proposed that consciousness was simply a property of matter that emerged when neurological systems became complex enough. These so-called emergent evolutionists pointed out that each successive unit of biochemical organization, from atom to molecule to cell and so on, exhibited properties that were not necessarily predictable from the behavior of their component parts. The wetness of the water molecule, for example, could not be logically derived from knowledge of the characteristics of the individual hydrogen and oxygen molecules composing it. Similarly, the metabolism of the cell was greater than the sum of its molecules. In this manner, emergent evolutionists made the case that consciousness could exhibit entirely different properties from the physical brain yet still be produced by it.

While some scientists wondered about the evolution of the mind, others began to take a more anatomical interest in mapping the terra incognita within the skull. Meticulous investigators dissected the brains of cadavers, microscopically examined brain tissues, analyzed and sketched neurons, and identified the ways in which the body's billions of nerve cells are knitted together to form the brain and nervous system. As the twentieth century waxed, the results of these investigations lent weight to the materialistic argument, which came into fullest flower in the mid-1950s with the hypothesis known as the mind-brain identity theory.

Identity theorists confirmed and extended the conviction of earlier materialists, namely that mental events are absolutely identical with neural events. That is, every thought or emotion a person experiences is generated by the electrochemical firing of neurons in the brain. The most ardent identity theorists contended that in time, science would pin open the mind in the way that anatomy students pinned open frogs or worms. When the underlying electrochemical patterns were drawn, it would be seen that each mental state corresponds to a particular pattern of physical activity. In short, they believed the mind to be nothing more than an ephemeral echo of the physical brain. In that sense, identity theorists said, mentation is no more mysterious than digestion. It is just an ordinary function of the healthy brain, and one need look no further than the strictly material realm to explain it.

The identity theory seemed enormously reasonable. It showed how a specific chain of events starting at the level of the cell and spreading by electrical signals along particular neuron networks of the nervous system could yield a specific mental state. And experiments had shown that a damaged brain can "learn" to use alternate neurological networks to produce that same mental state. For example, a person whose language center was damaged by a stroke might eventually speak again as different areas of the brain began to compensate for that one area's loss of function.

Even though the identity theory seems to offer a logical explanation of a complex process, according to some interested parties it does not address all aspects of the mind-brain debate. Australian physiologist Sir John Eccles contends that materialism's most firmly held article of faith, namely that neural events generate consciousness, simply begs the question. If all mental conditions are the result of physical neurological events, asks Eccles, how is it that the mental state thus engendered—say, anger—can in turn produce the physical effects on the body—such as increased blood pressure, tensed muscles, and internal temperature changes—that accompany anger?

Furthermore, he observes, materialism ignores the existence of such concepts as human will and free choice—forces that many of the world's religions and philosophies

insist affect human behavior. The radical materialistic argument that mental events only appear to influence human behavior strikes Eccles, a former materialist turned dualist, as absurd. He insists that any theory of consciousness must deal with not only the brain's effect on the mind but also the mind's impact on the brain.

Eccles is far from alone in his criticism of strict materialism. While still upholding the spirit of the materialistic doctrine, some neuroscientists have identified qualities of the mind that defy reduction to the purely physical. Hungarian neuroscientist János Szentágothai, a dyed-in-the-wool materialist, is one such example. Over the course of his career, Szentágothai made key contributions to the study of the physiology of the central nervous system. In the 1970s he plunged into the philosophical issues surrounding consciousness. As a materialist, Szentágothai stated he could not imagine "any material (or non-material) substrate of my own inner self except the roughly 50 billion nerve cells" with their countless interconnections.

Yet at the same time, the Hungarian accepts that his mental "self" has the power to influence the activities of those thronging nerve cells in ways that are not yet understood. Somehow, Szentágothai suspects, the potential for consciousness is built into the essence of the brain cells. "I do not think," he writes, "that consciousness or even self-awareness starts with man. Its rudiments have to be there with the very existence of the 'neural.' " No neuroscientist, he states, "could claim that she or he completely

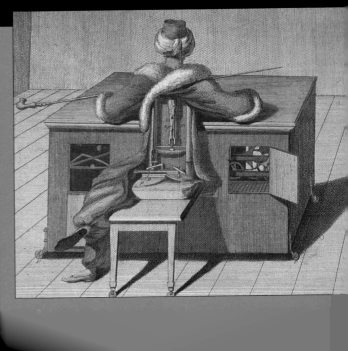

understands or can even correctly define the term mind."

In their search for answers to this dilemma, some disillusioned materialists have embraced a modified dualism. In a controversial 1977 book entitled *The Mind and Its Brain,* Eccles and his countryman, philosopher Sir Karl Popper, argue that in addition to brain states determined by physical laws, there are also mental states, which fall outside the boundaries of the material world yet interact with it. The authors posit three different worlds of reality and assert that what they call Worlds 2 and 3 should be considered every bit as real as World 1.

World 1 is the realm of physical objects, "of rocks and trees and physical fields of force." World 2 is the psychological realm, including the sensations produced by the senses—sight, sound, smell, taste, and touch—as well as thoughts, memories, dreams, imaginings, and other subjective experiences. Communication flows back and forth between Worlds 1 and 2 and results in World 3, the "products of the human mind": art, music, books, scientific theories—including, Popper adds wryly, "mistaken theories."

As a way of linking the worlds of physical and mental reality, Eccles, like Descartes, has located a place within the brain where the worlds of flesh and spirit interact. Descartes chose the pineal gland, but Eccles looked to a small tangle of nerves in the cerebral cortex named the supplementary motor area, or SMA. Experiments have shown that in the split second before an individual makes a voluntary movement—in the instant following a reader's mental decision to turn this page, say—a flurry of nerve impulses issue from the SMA. Eccles infers that this sudden surge of activity must be spawned by the arrival of signals from the nonmaterial mind.

Another significant experiment, by Danish neurophysiologist Per Roland, bolsters this inference. Roland showed that just before a light touch is applied to a finger of a subject who is watching the action, there is an increased flow of blood in the part of the brain that receives signals from the fingers. The increase, says Roland, must result from the subject's purely mental expectation of the touch—proof that mental activity produces physical activity.

Materialist holdouts argue that in suggesting the reality of a nonmaterial mind, Eccles and others have crossed into the territory of religion. In drawing the proper limits of their discipline, most scientists would agree in principle with the dictum of psychologist Donald Hebb. "The idea of an immaterial mind controlling the body is vitalism, no more, no less," he writes, "it has no place in science." Vitalism is the Aristotelian notion that a vital principle, or life force, flows in all living things—a theory that scientists have long denounced. Even Szentágothai, who admires the metaphorical power of Eccles and Popper's three-world model, maintains that to take the idea seriously "we should have to leave the domain of legitimate science and enter that of religion and faith."

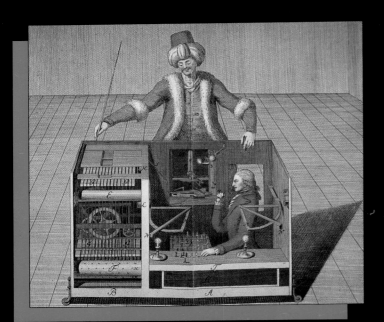

These eighteenth-century watercolors reveal the mechanical innards of the Phony Turk, a pipe-smoking, chess-playing automaton run by a man concealed beneath the robot's table. Some scientists and philosophers of the era concluded that the human mind was not qualitatively different from an automaton, since both were essentially machines. The only difference, said Frenchman Julien Offroy de La Mettrie, was that the mind was an "organic" machine rather than one constructed out of nuts and bolts.

Yet in allowing the possibility that the mind harbors a spiritual component, Eccles is in good historical company. For even while the materialists have vigorously pressed their case for the past 300 years, other scientists have less noisily taken the position that the exclusively materialistic description of the universe is shortsighted and that the explanation of a phenomenon in physical terms did not preclude its explanation in other terms. In other words, they have held the heretical position that science might not be the sole route to truth.

For example, the eighteenth-century German philosopher and mathematician Gottfried Wilhelm Leibniz, codiscoverer with Isaac Newton of calculus, suspected a metaphysical reality beyond the physical world. Space and time, mass, motion, and energy, Leibniz said, are merely intellectual constructs masking the underlying truth. William James, in his search to redefine consciousness, thought that the brain acted as a screen and filtered out a limited set of perceptions from a larger reality. Henri-Louis Bergson, an energetic and imaginative French philosopher who won a Nobel Prize for literature in 1928, agreed that the brain's main function was to pare down reality. That reality, he suggested, ultimately consisted of a ''vital impulse'' that could be grasped only by intuition.

Similarly, the eminent psychiatrist Carl Jung would not be bound by the physicists' strict definition of reality. In his monumental investigations of the mind, Jung paid particular attention to the zones just beyond the grasp of waking consciousness. Like Sigmund Freud, Jung expounded the importance of each human's unconscious mind, whose shadowy drives he believed shape behavior and yet are accessible to scrutiny only through creative outlets, such as dreams, fantasies, or artwork, and then only in symbolic terms. Jung's analysis of his own dreams and those of his colleagues and psychiatric patients led him to assert the existence of still another, broader type of unconscious, which he called the collective unconscious.

By Jung's reckoning, the collective unconscious belonged to all humankind. It was expressed in archetypes— or primitive symbols—myths, and folk tales with common themes and forms that could be found in every culture in every age. These potent images and stories, according to Jung, were not honed through individual experience but were the common inheritance of the species. In his writings, Jung sometimes endowed the collective unconscious with a paranormal power to foreshadow events. He believed, for instance, that a series of dreams he experienced toward the end of 1913, which were filled with images of flailing bodies drowning in seas of blood, presaged the global conflict that broke out in Europe the following year. In Jung's bold interpretations, the definition of the mind achieved a vast new dimension that transcended the scope of the materialist-dualist battle line.

Another farseeing Western effort to understand consciousness and eliminate the philosophical conflicts arising out of the classical dualistic and monistic ways of parsing the world was that of the renowned British mathematician and philosopher Alfred North Whitehead. One of Europe's leading thinkers in the years between the two world wars—and by all accounts a gentle and compassionate man—Whitehead created an elegant and formidable critique of reality called process philosophy. Although this difficult thesis defies paraphrasing, it holds, broadly, that space, time, and matter are intricately concocted abstractions, related to, but not equal to, reality. Whitehead saw reality, which is to say all that is, as being contrived from many interlocking fragments; no single aspect of reality could stand on its own. ''There are no whole truths,'' wrote Whitehead, ''all truths are half-truths. It is trying to treat them as whole truths that plays the devil.''

Human consciousness consists principally of ''actual entities,'' which are momentary experiences taking place in the present tense. These experiences derive from a category of ''potentialities,'' the infinite set of all things that are, as well as of those things that ''are not but might have been.'' The function of human consciousness is to grasp and unify as many actual entities as possible and transform them into

The fathers of evolutionary theory, Charles Darwin (left) and Alfred Russel Wallace (below), diverged in their views on the mind. Darwin argued that human mental capacities were the product of natural selection. His friend and colleague rejected this premise as "utterly inconceivable." Wallace asserted that there had to be a spiritual dimension to the mind that could not be explained by science. Darwin, in turn, was grieved by this appraisal, considering it a betrayal of their common hypothesis. He wrote to Wallace: "I hope you have not murdered too completely your own and my child."

Freud's Little Secret

At the turn of the twentieth century, Sigmund Freud transformed the study of psychology—up till then a woefully haphazard occupation—into a modern science. In the process, he proposed the first comprehensive theory of the human mind and offered plausible explanations for previously baffling mental disorders. Unbeknown to most of his contemporaries, however, he also dabbled in the occult.

Freud was trained as a neurologist, and he always considered himself first and foremost a scientist. But he had sufficient curiosity about the paranormal to join societies for psychical research in England and in the United States. There is also evidence that he conducted a number of experiments in telepathy.

The Viennese physician found it plausible that people might exchange thoughts and feelings without communicating them overtly, and he cited as proof the insightfulness of certain fortunetellers. He recalled a female patient who had visited a seer and had been told to expect to bear two children before turning thirty-two years of age. The prediction was incorrect, but it revealed—at least to Freud's satisfaction—the fortuneteller's ability to decipher his patient's feelings. This patient, he explained, had been unusually close to her father, and her mother had given birth to two babies when she was thirty-two. Freud deduced that the seer must have sensed the woman's desire to be like her mother—who, after all, had married the most important man in the patient's life.

Freud did not publicize his feelings about such matters for fear of being discredited as a quack. Nevertheless, near the end of his life he professed: "It would be a great satisfaction to me if I could convince myself and others on unimpeachable evidence of the existence of telepathic processes."

memories, which, taken together, make up a person's sense of self. For Whitehead, the universe is constantly changing, and reality is a mesh of endless, interrelated transformations. "Our minds are finite," wrote Whitehead, "and yet even in these circumstances of finitude we are surrounded by possibilities that are infinite, and the purpose of human life is to grasp as much as we can out of that infinitude."

In eschewing the mind-body split favored by Western dualism, Whitehead's difficult philosophy shows a striking similarity to certain aspects of Eastern thought and religion. For Buddhists, who freely acknowledge the metaphysical aspects of human consciousness, the analysis of human mentality has always involved a recognition of the central paradox of perception: The world of the body and objects, which appears so concrete, is illusory. True reality is accessible to contemplation but cannot be sounded by physical means. Nor can it be divided into subjects and objects, observers and things observed. Instead, true reality flows through the universe in an undifferentiated web.

An evocative illustration of this vision is found in the *Avatamsaka Sutra,* the Buddhist text set down sometime around the second or third century AD. The sutra describes a magical feature of the palace of Indra, the King of Heaven. Over the palace, the sutra reports, hangs a vast network of pearls so artfully arranged that by gazing at any one of the pearls, a viewer is able simultaneously to see the reflections of all the others. To interpreters of Buddhist thought, Indra's cleverly configured net symbolizes the spiritual interconnectedness of all things in the infinite universe.

The teachings of Hinduism also extol the existence of a truth beyond immediate perception that is similar to the Buddhist dharmakaya, the melding of the mind and the material world. The Hindus call it Brahman, the essence of the universe. It is impersonal and dimensionless, although it fills space. It is basically inaccessible to human awareness,

"Wholly unconscious of what it meant,"
Swiss psychiatrist Carl Jung painted his first
mandala (above) in 1916. He later conclud-
ed that such "magic circles" were instinctive
renderings of a universal symbol that people
have been drawing for 20,000 years. Creat-
ing mandalas, he wrote, tapped directly into
"the microcosmic nature of the psyche,"
bringing to light an individual's repressed
and forgotten life experiences. He consid-
ered the process so enlightening that he
made painting and interpreting mandalas
part of his treatment for many patients.

Albin MICHEL
ÉDITEUR
22, rue Huyghens, 22
PARIS (14e)

LE PETIT INVENTEUR

ABONNEMENTS :
FRANCE...... **12** francs
ÉTRANGER.. **18** francs

LES ONDES HUMAINES

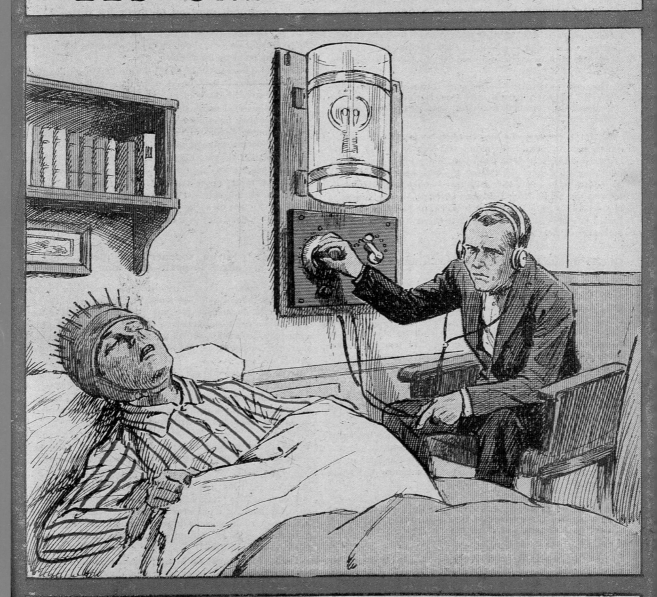

La pensée humaine émet des **radiations** qu'enregistre la T. S. F.

An intent researcher adjusts a knob on a fanciful radio receiver designed to measure brain waves—presumably conducted through the subject's spiked cap—in this futuristic 1928 cover drawing from a popular French science magazine. The picture illustrated an article speculating that sophisticated radio technology might one day allow a listener to eavesdrop on another person's thoughts.

which is blinded by the mind's built-in tendency to compartmentalize, categorize, name, and reason. These mental qualities, Hindus believe, separate the mind from the undifferentiated Brahman.

The great Eastern philosophy called Taoism admits the truth of the objective world while also proclaiming a holistic view. In exploring the nature of consciousness and of the universe, Taoism emphasizes that the world of appearances is complemented by another world, one of non-being, and that behind these two worlds lies an even deeper reality called the Tao. It is an elusive concept that can be grasped only by indirection or paradox. The eternal Tao is constantly in flux, and its followers must be in tune with its unpredictable flow. The enlightened person, says the basic text of Taoism, the *Tao-te ching*, will "Act without action. Do without ado." He or she understands that "To yield is to be preserved whole. To be bent is to become straight. To be empty is to be full. To be worn out is to be renewed."

Despite their mystical aspects, the Buddhist, Hindu, and Taoist views of consciousness and the cosmos show astonishing parallels to the new vision of the universe unveiled by the investigations of twentieth-century physicists. Fritjof Capra was among the first Western scientists to explore the implausible parallels between ancient mysticism and modern physics. In 1975 he wrote in *The Tao of Physics*, "The basic oneness of the universe is not only the central characteristic of the mystical experience, but is also one of the most important revelations of modern physics. It becomes apparent at the atomic level and manifests itself more and more as one penetrates deeper into matter, down into the realm of subatomic particles."

The principal architects of modern physics were Albert Einstein and Niels Bohr, who succeeded in overthrowing classical Newtonian physics as it applied both to the very large and to the very small. Newton's solid and predictable universe had come to be replaced by a far more tenuous and quirky cosmos. In the early decades of the twentieth century, Einstein showed that energy and matter were simply different forms of the same thing, which could be translated into one or the other form in calculable proportions. In his theories, Einstein revealed that space and time were also inextricably related, and he argued that the size of any object or the duration of any event was relative, depending entirely on where the observer stood.

Meanwhile, Niels Bohr and German physicist Werner Heisenberg eyed the atom and discovered that it was less substantial than earlier physicists had supposed. It was impossible, they showed mathematically, to calculate with any certainty where in a given atom a particular electron would be at a given moment. Instead, an electron's position could be stated only in terms of probabilities, as a matter of the likelihood that it would be in a certain place at a certain time.

So slippery is the footing on the playground of quantum physics, in fact, that some scientists have had to conclude that the very presence of human consciousness affects the train of events on the subatomic level. Indeed, it appears that human perception, having the power to change reality by observing it, constitutes an integral part of the universe. In describing the quantum universe's interconnected web, of which human consciousness is a part, Capra wrote, "None of the properties of any part of this web is fundamental; they all follow from the properties of the other parts, and the overall consistency of their mutual interrelations determines the structure of the entire web."

In noting the paradoxical confluence of ancient mysticism and modern physics, German theologian and philosopher Rudolph Otto drew an intriguing correlation. He suggested that the urge to find out about the world—the motivating force for a scientist—is rooted in the mystical intuition that a oneness lies behind the physical world's multiplicity. Now, it seems, after centuries of pursuing divergent paths, the methods of the mystic and the scientist are converging.

If the universe is nondeterministic, as modern physics claims, and if all nature flows through an interpenetrating web, then there is no basis for the classical divisions of ob-

The Buddha's face radiates the sublime peace of enlightenment in this fifth-century sculpture. The spiritual quest of the Indian prince-turned-holy man resulted in a radically new way of thinking about human consciousness: Instead of revering the intellect, devout Buddhists seek to rise above its distractions. Ultimate awareness, they believe, flowers only when one has overcome the mind's hum of activity.

Neurosurgeon Wilder Penfield came to doubt that the mind would ever be understood purely through study of the brain. He illustrated this view with a rock painting in which a broken line links the Greek word for spirit with the symbols of science and the brain.

the new science of holography, a method of creating images using lasers. To form an image, light from the laser is split into two beams. One beam is directed toward the object to be photographed and the other is aimed toward a mirror. Both beams then reflect onto a photosensitive plate or film, which produces a chaotic-looking mass of light and dark swirls. Although this pattern appears confused when viewed with the naked eye, a stunning transformation takes place when the hologram is illuminated by a laser beam: An image appears of the object photographed that remains convincingly three-dimensional when viewed from different angles. A further, significant attribute of a hologram is that each small bit of holographic film contains virtually the same information as the whole. If a hologram on a photographic plate were to shatter, the entire image could be reconstituted from even a square centimeter of the original.

Pribram's studies convinced him that the brain stored information in much the same way, that is, not in specific spatial division but distributed over the entire neural network. Human brains, he proposes, exhibit the same properties as holograms, not only in creating a three-dimensional version of the world from electrochemical impulses from the senses but also in spreading information across the entire system, so that even if portions of the brain are damaged, the functions performed by those parts of the brain or the memories stored there are preserved.

But, having decided the brain was a hologram, Pribram was stymied, because his model still left him asking who was looking at the hologram, reconstituting it, as it were, into three dimensions. Pribram puzzled over this problem and concluded that he must be asking the wrong question. Perhaps there *was* no objective world that was being rebuilt in the brain. Perhaps the universe itself was also holographic and the "lenses" of the senses were, like a reconstituting laser beam, endowing it with a ghostly yet convincing dimensionality. Excited by this conjecture, Pribram by chance learned of the musings of physicist David Bohm, who had made a rather convincing case for the holographic organization of the universe.

ject and subject, mind and body. The insights of the new physics demand a more holistic view of consciousness, and some daring thinkers have attempted to forge a bold, synthetic vision of human awareness. One of the most exciting holistic hypotheses to emerge in recent years is that advanced by two Americans, neuroscientist Karl Pribram, who heads Radford University's Center for Brain Research and Information Sciences in Radford, Virginia, and physicist David Bohm, emeritus professor of theoretical physics at Birkbeck College, University of London.

Like so many others, Pribram began his career as a strict materialist in the 1940s but gradually accepted the idea that the mind might be more than the product of brain activity. He became intrigued with a concept suggested by

Bohm argued that the deep reality of the universe is enfolded, invisible to observation by classical scientific means. Through mathematical modeling and analogy, Bohm had glimpsed a reality akin to the Eastern concepts of dharmakaya, Brahman, or Tao; as he put it, an "intangible, invisible flux" of "inseparable interconnectedness." To Bohm, the idea of a stable world of normal consciousness was an illusion. The universe, in his estimation, was kaleidoscopic and dynamic, in a state of being that he dubbed the "holomovement."

Pribram took the critical step of fusing his idea of the holographic mind with Bohm's holographic universe and created a theory of consciousness with metaphysical implications, boldly bridging the moat between science and religion. Pribram proposed that classical thinkers had been misguided in trying to sort out the differences between mind and body; as the mystics proclaimed, belief in such a split was delusive. Consciousness, Pribram said, was an extension of the larger, hidden reality. Mental properties were not an anomalous, ineffable part of the material world; they were, he wrote in a 1978 essay titled "What the Fuss Is All About," the "pervasive organizing principles of the universe, which includes the brain."

Pribram's theory brings Western thinking close indeed to Eastern mysticism, dissolving distinctions between mental and physical, spiritual and material. In the holographic domain, Pribram explains, "What is organism (with its component organs) is no longer sharply distinguished from what lies outside the boundaries of the skin. In the holographic domain, each organism represents in some manner the universe, and each portion of the universe represents in some manner the organisms within it."

In 1949 Jorge Luis Borges, the brilliant, blind, Argentine writer, published a short story called "The Aleph." The tale describes a narrator's discovery, in the basement of a house in Buenos Aires, of the magical Aleph, "one of the points in space that contains all of the other points."

More than a geometric or optical oddity, the imaginary Aleph, measuring about an inch in diameter, turns out to be a window into the boundless, ever-changing universe. Through it the awe-struck narrator viewed, "in a single gigantic instant," everything that has ever happened or will happen. Past, present, and future "occupied the same point in space, without overlapping or transparency." Grappling to recount what he saw, the narrator then lists in series the impressions that had in fact rushed simultaneously into his consciousness:

"Each thing (a mirror's face, let's say) was infinite things, since I distinctly saw it from every angle of the universe. I saw the teeming sea; I saw daybreak and nightfall; I saw the multitudes of America; I saw a silvery cobweb in the center of a black pyramid; I saw a splintered labyrinth (it was London). . . . I saw bunches of grapes, snow, tobacco, lodes of metal, steam; I saw convex equatorial deserts and each one of their grains of sand; I saw a woman in Inverness whom I shall never forget. . . . I saw a sunset in Querétaro that seemed to reflect the color of a rose in Bengal. . . . I saw horses with flowing manes on a shore of the Caspian Sea at dawn; I saw the delicate bone structure of a hand. . . . I saw in a showcase in Mirzapur a pack of Spanish playing cards; I saw the slanting shadows of ferns on a greenhouse floor; I saw tigers, pistons, bisons, tides, and armies; I saw all the ants on the planet. . . . I saw the circulation of my own dark blood. . . . and I felt dizzy and wept, for my eyes had seen that secret and conjectured object whose name is common to all men but which no man has looked upon—the unimaginable universe."

In a fictional frame, Borges's story seems to blend parts of Bohm's and Pribram's holographic visions of universe and mind, which were not developed until later, as well as the old Eastern mystics' notion of Indra's fabulous reflecting pearls. It is almost as if all these disparate consciousnesses were themselves peering into a hologram—viewing an image of which, in turn, they were each a part. Perhaps in this mutual mirroring of art, science, and mysticism there glimmers a hint of understanding of that most puzzling of entities, the human mind.

Seeing Clues in an Unseen Light

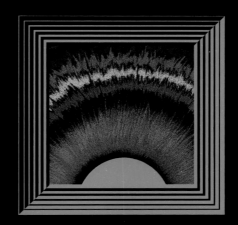

$\mathbf{T}$he aura is the weathervane of the soul," wrote American psychic Edgar Cayce. Like others over the years, Cayce declared that he could actually perceive the aura, said to be a three-dimensional nimbus of glowing colored energy emanating from every living thing, plant or animal. Believers in the aura say that it provides insight into an individual's health, emotions, and psychological attitudes—or, as Cayce put it, "the way the winds of destiny are blowing" for that person.

Doctors in ancient Persia purportedly diagnosed physical illness by studying the light they discerned surrounding their patients. Sixteenth-century Swiss physician and alchemist Paracelsus wrote that he observed signs of health or disease in the "luminous sphere" radiating from human beings. Today, aura interpreters report that both mental and physical problems manifest themselves in the body's swathe of colored light. Others find clues to spiritual development, believing that a brilliant aura reflects an enlightened being. Modern enthusiasts argue that the halos of holy figures in old paintings are not simply artistic conventions, but auras. Contemporary aura readers tell of bright light enveloping people who are in harmony with themselves and the world.

The following pages reveal a system of interpretation developed by Barbara Bowers of San Diego, a self-described aura consultant. Her method focuses on personality and individual potential. Moreover, according to Bowers, it can also tell you the color of your own aura—and what it means.

The Many Hues of Personality

In Barbara Bowers's system of aura interpretation, the band of light closest to the body is the personality color, the core aura developed at birth and usually kept for life. Bowers says this band is always one of fourteen colors or combinations of colors, each indicating a different way of relating to the world. (The bands outside the personality color, discussed on pages 32 and 33, allegedly reveal other truths.)

Bowers calls the personality color the "code that determines how we grapple with the main issues of our lives." It sheds light upon actions, beliefs, strengths, weaknesses, and compatibility with others; understanding it can lead to greater fulfillment in life: "When individuals are able to focus their energies in the direction in which their soul-river is flowing, they are able to identify opportunities that are

PHYSICAL (BODY) FAMILY

Yellow and Physical Tan constitute the physical (body) family of personality colors. Bowers says people with these colors take cues about the world from their bodies. Before they consider a situation intellectually or respond to it emotionally, they experience a physical reaction such as sweaty palms, increased heart rate, or nervous fidgeting.

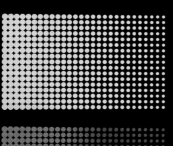

YELLOW
Yellows have the most childlike personalities of all, Bowers says. Sociable, active, and fun-loving, they revel in physical joys. But their bodies are highly sensitive to pain, sometimes causing them to fall prey to physical addictions in their efforts to soothe themselves.

PHYSICAL TAN
Physical Tans are the enigmas of the spectrum. Silent and inward turning, they tend to be rigid thinkers with little ability to share their feelings with others, let alone with themselves. When they do open up, however, their intimacy is particularly intense.

PHYSICAL (ENVIRONMENT) FAMILY

Red, Orange, and Magenta make up the physical (environment) family of personality colors. People in this group experience life as physical reality. In order to grapple with an idea, they must be able to give it tangible form. According to Barbara Bowers, action is crucial to these individuals, and they live with "gusto, verve, and courage."

RED
Literal-minded, hardworking, and generous, Reds are pragmatists who thrive when tasks require physical prowess. They love nature, deal with feelings straightforwardly, and are usually optimistic. But their explosive tempers make them potentially violent.

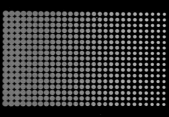

ORANGE
Oranges "shake their fists in the face of God," Bowers says. Their daredevil existence revolves around one life-and-death challenge after another, leaving little time for relationships or other forms of personal development.

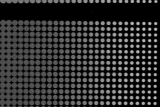

MAGENTA
Magentas are nonconformists. Individualistic rather than rebellious, they burgeon with an offbeat creativity that seems bizarre to some. Bowers advises them to resist temptations to hide their differences: Their uniqueness is the source of their identity.

Like Edgar Cayce and many others who have claimed to see auras, Barbara Bowers says that throughout her childhood she assumed that everyone perceived the bands of color surrounding human bodies. After years of seeing auras, she decided to explain her system of interpretation in her book, What Color Is Your Aura?

uniquely theirs and to act with poise and self-assurance." Five of the fourteen types of personality bands that Bowers claims to perceive are unusual hues or color combinations to which she has attached special names. Mental Tan, a rich honey gold, is so called to distinguish it from three double colors that also have "tan" in their names. Physical Tan, Nurturing Tan, and Loving Tan are each made up of a band of Mental Tan immediately surrounding the body and a second ring of color—green, blue, or red, respectively—outside the tan. Crystal, the fifth unusual color, is "a gossamer, foglike mist with other colors in it."

Descriptions of the personality colors—which Bowers groups by similar traits into four families—appear below. To find out what yours is, see pages 36 and 37.

MENTAL FAMILY

A personality color from the mental family is said to signify a cerebral approach to the world. Individuals who fall into this category think tirelessly and perceive reality through thoughts and ideas, which they love to play with and organize. Their greatest challenge in life is attempting to handle the seeming irrationality of emotion.

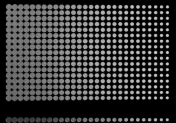

MENTAL TAN
Logical thinking is the hallmark of the Mental Tans. Their humming minds operate methodically. They may seem pedantic to others, says Bowers, while they themselves may be perplexed and disturbed by their feelings, which exist outside their intellectual bailiwick.

GREEN
With their razor-sharp, analytical minds, Greens often leave others in the dust of their fast-paced creativity. They strive for perfection out of fear of inadequacy. Their happiness depends on voluminous productivity; Bowers says they see life as "a giant 'to do' list."

NURTURING TAN
Nurturing Tans are the good samaritans of the world, offering others emotional support, physical aid, and altruistic kindness. They marry a dedication to humanity with acute intelligence, a pairing that produces concrete results.

LOVING TAN
Loving Tans feel a deep love for humanity. Yet they hesitate to carry this affection to a personal level: Since childhood, most have been rejected because of their maddening disorganization.

EMOTIONAL/SPIRITUAL FAMILY

People whose personality colors fall in the emotional/spiritual family prefer hopes, wishes, and dreams to tangible reality. They value emotions as well as feelings and perform at their peak when they are able to rely upon intuition rather than upon logic. In their ephemeral realm, "abstraction has more reality than does paying the bills."

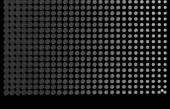

BLUE
Blues live to serve others. However, they approach life purely emotionally, guided by their keen intuition. Logical thought processes confuse them, and they have trouble making decisions. Further, they lack the assertiveness to ask that their own needs be met.

VIOLET
Passionate and somewhat egotistical, Violets possess the intelligence and intuition required to "make a significant difference" in the world. Guilt and fear sometimes hinder their quest for achievement, but ultimately they are able to realize their dreams.

LAVENDER
Bowers says Lavenders seem always to be suffering from "a kind of jet lag." Caught between their own fantasy worlds and the intrusive demands of the real world, they are open to paranormal experiences. Their rich daydreams fuel magical artistic creations.

CRYSTAL
Directly linked to a higher power, Crystals have special healing powers, Bowers reports. Despite this divine connection, they find the world harsh and cold. They have no instinct about social behavior, so they copy peers, actually adopting other colors into their auras.

INDIGO
According to Bowers, Indigo appeared as a personality color only recently. She says these children and young adults will become the leaders of a new age because they were born with an innate omniscience. They are free of the problems that plague other people.

Insights from the Outer Bands

The mantle of colored light that allegedly surrounds human beings extends far beyond the personality color. In addition to that primary layer, the aura boasts five to seven others. These outer bands vary in number and color over the course of life, and they disclose information about events, feelings, and priorities.

Bowers divides what she calls the auric bands into three groups. The first contains the personality color, what she dubs an overlay, if there is one, and a spirituality band. The overlay is a second personality color that may radiate around the head and shoulders outside the primary band. It adds another group of characteristics—which may be quite different from the first—to the mix of an individual's personality. Outside that is the spirituality band, consisting of a white space, the width of which reveals the degree of a person's spiritual growth.

Bowers calls the second group the drive bands. These layers, three or four in number, show resentment or contentment with some aspect of one's life. They may also refer to the planning or execution of projects or to the status of a personal goal.

The outermost layers of the aura are called the power bands. They express a person's way of handling authority. The first band in this group is usually red and indicates by its size and by the depth of its color how a person was treated early in life. The second layer sheds light upon how one leads others, and the final band divulges an individual's feelings about romantic relationships.

Colors that frequently emerge in the outer bands and the meanings that Bowers ascribes to them appear at right.

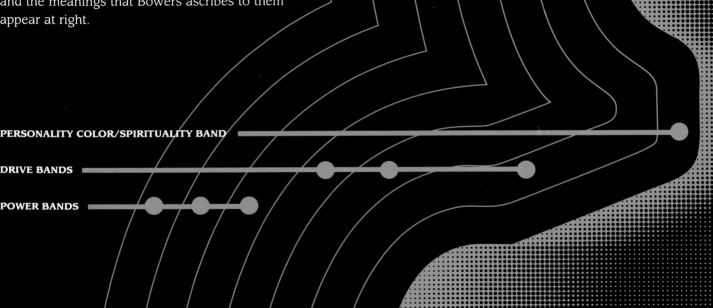

PERSONALITY COLOR/SPIRITUALITY BAND

DRIVE BANDS

POWER BANDS

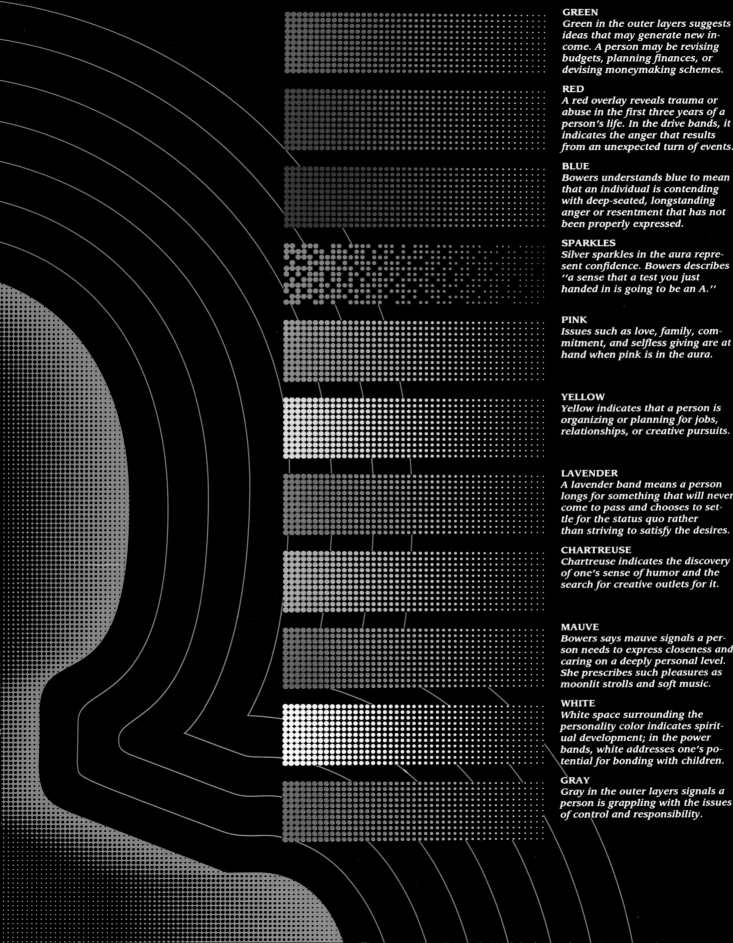

GREEN
Green in the outer layers suggests ideas that may generate new income. A person may be revising budgets, planning finances, or devising moneymaking schemes.

RED
A red overlay reveals trauma or abuse in the first three years of a person's life. In the drive bands, it indicates the anger that results from an unexpected turn of events.

BLUE
Bowers understands blue to mean that an individual is contending with deep-seated, longstanding anger or resentment that has not been properly expressed.

SPARKLES
Silver sparkles in the aura represent confidence. Bowers describes ''a sense that a test you just handed in is going to be an A.''

PINK
Issues such as love, family, commitment, and selfless giving are at hand when pink is in the aura.

YELLOW
Yellow indicates that a person is organizing or planning for jobs, relationships, or creative pursuits.

LAVENDER
A lavender band means a person longs for something that will never come to pass and chooses to settle for the status quo rather than striving to satisfy the desires.

CHARTREUSE
Chartreuse indicates the discovery of one's sense of humor and the search for creative outlets for it.

MAUVE
Bowers says mauve signals a person needs to express closeness and caring on a deeply personal level. She prescribes such pleasures as moonlit strolls and soft music.

WHITE
White space surrounding the personality color indicates spiritual development; in the power bands, white addresses one's potential for bonding with children.

GRAY
Gray in the outer layers signals a person is grappling with the issues of control and responsibility.

A Sampler of the Aura Reader at Work

Barbara Bowers believes that many children perceive auras but that they usually drop the gift because their elders reprimand them for reporting the phenomenon. Even as adults, she says, some people possess an untapped visual sensitivity to the nimbus. She advises, however, that no one read an aura without careful consideration: Serious issues that beginners may not know how to handle sometimes surface.

Bowers says she sees auras by using her peripheral vision. She begins by reading the bands closest to the body—believing them to contain the most salient information—then moves outward. She says the aura has texture, sound, size, shape, and color, which contribute to her understanding. Four of her readings appear below, with silhouettes representing the people she studied.

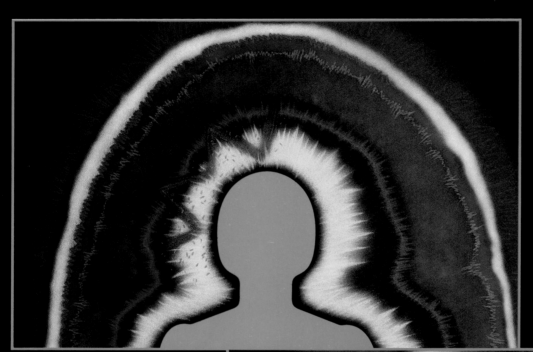

The aura Bowers sees around a twenty-seven-year-old male reveals he is a fun-loving Yellow. The gray jags over his right shoulder declare heterosexuality, and the pink band encircling the yellow suggests a new romance. The chartreuse band means he is opening himself to genuine joy and laughter for the first time in years, although he does not fully trust this instinct yet, as the faintness of the color relates. The blue band divulges his anger against a demanding parent, feeling he has spent too much of his life trying to live up to another's expectations. Bowers counsels that he should express these sentiments—if only to himself—since she believes that unresolved resentment can produce illness. The dark red line encircles the man's body, showing that just one of his parents nurtured him. The white band indicates he is not ready to bond with children. And the band of pink discloses that he is open to intimate relationships but still has many things to learn before marriage.

An iconoclastic Magenta, the thirty-five-year-old woman whose aura appears at right experienced trauma early in life, says Bowers. A red overlay reveals that the pain she suffered during a difficult birth has made her defensive, and the red streak betrays a recent argument. The rich yellow suggests that the woman is working on a creative project. The deep pink band tells that people have criticized her for her unabashed expression of her sexuality, and this has shaken her self-esteem, as the gray band signals. She doubts her ability to make money, according to the faint green band, but she need not: The darker green outline ensures her success. The smooth red line reveals her parents' laissez-faire attitude about her upbringing. And the white band indicates she is not ready for children. The darker edge of pink divulges that this strongly individualistic woman will have trouble forming an emotional bond with those who try to confine her.

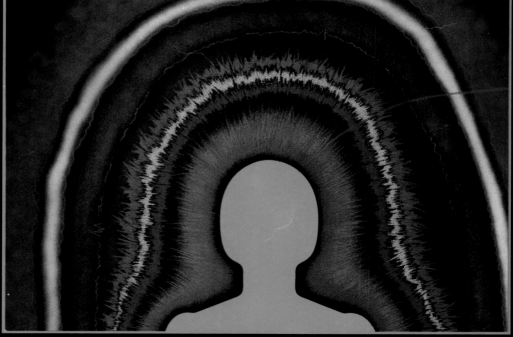

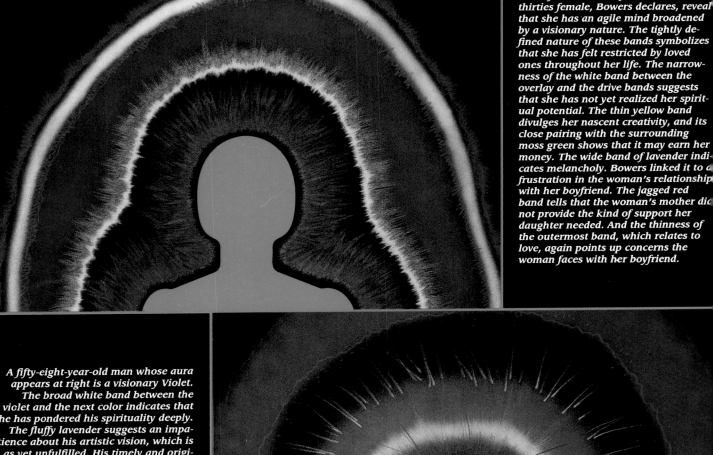

The green personality color and violet overlay in the aura of another mid-thirties female, Bowers declares, reveal that she has an agile mind broadened by a visionary nature. The tightly defined nature of these bands symbolizes that she has felt restricted by loved ones throughout her life. The narrowness of the white band between the overlay and the drive bands suggests that she has not yet realized her spiritual potential. The thin yellow band divulges her nascent creativity, and its close pairing with the surrounding moss green shows that it may earn her money. The wide band of lavender indicates melancholy. Bowers linked it to a frustration in the woman's relationship with her boyfriend. The jagged red band tells that the woman's mother did not provide the kind of support her daughter needed. And the thinness of the outermost band, which relates to love, again points up concerns the woman faces with her boyfriend.

A fifty-eight-year-old man whose aura appears at right is a visionary Violet. The broad white band between the violet and the next color indicates that he has pondered his spirituality deeply. The fluffy lavender suggests an impatience about his artistic vision, which is as yet unfulfilled. His timely and original creativity shines from the yellow stripes, as his professional confidence does from the silver sparkles: He knows his work is good. The red band is quite thin and dark, showing that he is no longer influenced by his upbringing. The pink relationship band is marked off by a boundary line, which means that the man's marriage has reached a limit beyond which further growth may be impossible. Bowers counsels that he may either leave the relationship or may seek from friends the support and stimulation that he does not receive from his wife. Maintaining the current state of the marriage, she says, will

4   I am OFTEN like this.

5   This is ME!

To begin the test, use a piece of paper to cover the colors that appear at the end of each of the fourteen rows of answer spaces. This way, your responses will not be influenced by what you already know about each personality color. Respond to each statement quickly, writing the number of your response in the appropriate answer space. Do not linger over the choices. If you have difficulty responding to a statement, your answer is probably "1" or "2."

After you complete the test, find the colors in which you have scored the highest by adding the numbers in each row of answer spaces. Go back to the groups of statements that apply to those colors and respond to each again, this time giving them more thought. Compute your scores a second time to determine your true personality color. A second significantly high score reveals that you have an overlay in addition to your main color. Keep in mind that each color has its inherent strengths and that no color is better than another.

THE QUESTIONNAIRE

1.   You are methodical in your thinking.

2.   You have a strong inner desire to make your mark on the world.

3.   You resent emotional and domestic demands made on you.

4.   Esoteric spiritual or political philosophies have great emotional and intellectual appeal for you.

5.   You seek the unusual or the avant-garde.

6.   You cry easily.

7.   You are not judgmental or critical of the ways in which others express their emotions or feelings.

8.   You are at ease in any environment where healing is the primary activity or occupation.

9.   When faced with a dangerous task, you carefully plan how to handle any crisis that may arise.

10.   You are a loner.

11.   When solving problems, you are able to visualize all the steps and the solution at the same time.

12.   You have no biases about sexuality—heterosexuality, bisexuality, or homosexuality.

13.   You prefer working at jobs that are physically demanding.

14.   You react physically (with sweaty palms, for example) before you respond to a situation mentally or emotionally.

15.   As a leader, you solicit lots of detailed information from others in order to make decisions.

24.   You are slow to choose friends.

25.   You do not require emotional loyalty to effectively mentor someone.

26.   In school, you learn most effectively in an unstructured environment.

27.   For you, sex is for physical pleasure.

28.   When you find yourself in a tense situation, you want to run away or pretend it does not exist.

29.   You have difficulty sharing your emotions and feelings with others.

30.   You would rather be the theorist of a project, and leave the building of the working model to someone else.

31.   You diagnose problems by recognizing patterns.

32.   You are a dreamer who likes to live in the fantasies you create.

33.   You are a spontaneous person.

34.   The experience of God's love is the spiritual force in your life.

35.   You look for ways to improve your community.

36.   You rarely show your deepest feelings.

37.   You prefer activities that allow you to demonstrate physical prowess.

38.   You evaluate objects by how solid or substantial they feel.

39.   You are attracted to religions with strong theological structures that allow for personal interpretation.

40.   You lead by forcing others to rethink and reexamine old beliefs, values, and ways of doing things.

41.   When you lose your temper, you get over it quickly.

42.   You are not cynical.

43.   You like social activities that combine business and pleasure.

44.   You are not "free and easy" when spending your money on others.

45.   You see God as the "brain" that created the universe.

46.   You express your sexuality creatively, intuitively, and experimentally.

47.   You are attracted to products that have unusual or unexpected design features.

48.   When looking for a job, you have difficulty asking for the salary you deserve.

49.   You feel that raising a well-educated child is the greatest contribution you can make to your community.

50.   You enjoy reading biographies and diaries that describe the lives

51. You prefer individual competition rather than team effort.

52. You are slow to commit to any belief system.

53. You eagerly seek to please those you love and care about.

54. You perceive spirituality to be in everything you do.

55. If you have enough money to buy the necessities, you are happy.

56. You experience God as the physical sensation of the joy of being alive.

57. You prefer a spiritual belief system that relies on a foundation of laws and principles.

58. You lead by telling people what to do.

59. You prefer a few specially chosen friends who stimulate you intellectually.

60. Your artistic pursuits often keep you indoors.

61. You form loose friendships that are not encumbered with bonds of expectation.

62. You feel more comfortable sharing the leadership by being a co-chairperson.

63. You financially support community groups and programs that benefit society.

64. Your source of personal power is your ability to mentally retreat inward.

65. You are not interested in organized religion or other belief systems.

66. You are meticulous in following instructions given to you by your supervisor.

67. You prefer social gatherings where you have an opportunity to talk to many different people.

68. You need to be awakened slowly from a sound sleep to avoid being irritable or in physical pain.

69. When playing a team sport, you rally the team when the chips are down.

70. You like parties.

71. To you, money is security.

72. You feel compelled to do something significant with your life.

73. You find great satisfaction in assisting people by giving ideas and information.

74. You prefer a somewhat isolated existence rather than one in which you would have to conform to society's expectations.

75. When you see something that you like, you choose to have your fantasy now and pay later.

76. You do not enjoy endurance sports such as cross-country skiing or weight-lifting.

77. You feel that spiritual principles must have practical application in the real world.

78. You prefer quiet, introspective, spiritual disciplines.

79. You prefer to work for a commission, or even as a freelancer, rather than for a regular, fixed salary.

80. You believe that to be a good leader, you must first be a good follower.

81. You have difficulty managing money effectively.

82. You cannot be coerced into doing something in which you are not interested.

83. You experience spirituality when you physically participate in the

84. You lead others with enthusiasm because you ... people.

85. You enjoy working with mechanical devices su... calculators, and stereo equipment.

86. Possessions are important to you as stepping-s... and influence.

87. To you, ideas are things, not mental abstractio...

88. You see ideas as three-dimensional patterns.

89. You express your spirituality through your stro... with nature.

90. When making a decision, you try to find a solu... please everyone.

91. You lead others by incorporating their feelings... making process.

92. You work best in an environment that is calm ... limited contact with others.

93. You do not need friends or social interaction to...

94. To you, money represents physical safety and s...

95. You have difficulty keeping track of personal p...

96. You are content to work with your hands.

97. You want to know how and why things work th...

98. You enjoy working in occupations that require...

1	15	29	43	57	71	85	
2	19	5	2	1	1	2	= 15

2	16	30	44	58	72	86	
3	4	2	3	1	2	1	= 17

3	17	31	45	59	73	87	
4	2	3	5	4	2	1	= 21

4	18	32	46	60	74	88	
4	3	4	1	1	3	1	= 18

5	19	33	47	61	75	89	
4	2	1	3	3	3	4	= 20

6	20	34	48	62	76	90	
1	5	2	5	4	2	4	= 22

7	21	35	49	63	77	91	
4	1	1	2	1	3	1	= 13

8	22	36	50	64	78	92	
3	5	5	4	5	5	5	= 32

9	23	37	51	65	79	93	
2	3	5	4	3	1	5	= 23

10	24	38	52	66	80	94	
5	5	2	2	2	2	1	= 17

11	25	39	53	67	81	95	
2	3	5	3	1	3	4	= 19

12	26	40	54	68	82	96	
5	3	4	4	2	3	4	= 25

13	27	41	55	69	83	97	
3	2	4	3	1	1	3	= 17

14	28	42	56	70	84	98	

CHAPTER 2

Windows into the Brain

iagnosed at various times in their lives as severely retarded, autistic, or psychotic, identical twins George and Charles might elicit little more than mild curiosity or even a momentary feeling of aversion from a stranger meeting them for the first time. In his 1987 book, *The Man Who Mistook His Wife for a Hat,* neurologist Oliver Sacks notes that the twins are "unprepossessing at first encounter—a sort of grotesque Tweedledum and Tweedledee . . . undersized, with disturbing disproportions in head and hands, high-arched palates, high-arched feet, monotonous squeaky voices, a variety of peculiar tics and mannerisms, and a very high generative myopia, requiring glasses so thick that their eyes seem distorted, giving them the appearance of absurd little professors." Professors they could never be, however. Though by then middle-aged—they were born in 1939—the twins had IQs that measured between sixty and seventy, equivalent to that of an eight- to ten-year-old child. They can read only a few simple words and must struggle to do even the most rudimentary addition and subtraction problems with any accuracy. The concepts of multiplication and division are entirely beyond their comprehension. When asked the product of seven times four, one of the twins replied, "two." When asked what seven times four meant, he answered, "It means fourteen."

Despite their physical and mental limitations, though, the twins possess some truly remarkable abilities. They can memorize 300-digit numbers with ease and often play a game together in which they exchange 8-, 9-, and even 20-digit prime numbers (numbers that cannot be evenly divided by a number other than themselves or one). If given a date within the last 40,000 years—or the next 40,000—they can state almost instantly the day of the week on which it falls. The twins can also describe, with uncanny accuracy, the minor events of any day in their lives from the time they were four years old. When a *LIFE* magazine reporter asked them on what day in 1960 a big snowstorm occurred, the answer came without hesitation: "On December 11, a Sunday, about two in the afternoon it started. The weather really went on a toot that day."

George and Charles owe the stark contrasts in their intelligence and ability to function to savant syndrome, an extremely rare condition in which a person with a serious mental handicap, such as severe retardation, autism, or schizophrenia, exhibits an astonishing ability or talent, usually in a single, narrowly defined area. Some savants share George's and Charles's phenomenal skills at calendar calculating. Others are able to perform an intricate Bach or Mozart composition on the piano after hearing it only once. Still others can memorize prodigious amounts of information, such as an entire telephone directory. Scientists do not yet fully understand how these strange skills develop in people like George and Charles, although they suspect it is somehow related to a particular type of brain damage that usually occurs before birth.

Savant syndrome is just one example of the mysterious relationship that exists between the brain, the physical organ of thought, and the mind, the mental process by which an individual feels, remembers, wills, and reasons. Damage to the brain, whether congenital or sustained after birth, frequently results in perplexing disorders of the mind. One man who suffered head injuries in an automobile accident, for instance, was no longer able to recognize faces—even his own in the mirror—although he could easily identify simple schematic objects, such as a watch or a key. A woman with a brain tumor acquired what German neurologists called *Witzel-sucht,* or ''joking disease,'' a fundamental sense that everything in life is facetious or insignificant. Scientists believe that the

study of such unusual conditions can lead to a better understanding of how the intangible elements of the mind—emotions and personality—are shaped by the physical workings of the brain.

The human brain is a complex mass of billions of nerve cells, or neurons, and a trillion supporting cells, known as neuroglia. Most of these cells can be found in the cerebral cortex, the wrinkled layer of pinkish gray matter that overlies the rest of the brain and that is believed to be the seat of consciousness and intellectual thought. Cells on the surface of the cerebral cortex process information received from the outside world through the body's senses. The data is then passed on to the interior of the cerebral cortex, where it is combined with information from memory and from other areas of the brain to create consciousness—the feelings, thoughts, images, and ideas that make up an individual's internal psychological world.

Scientists know that the transmission of information within the brain is accomplished by the neurons through electrical impulses. But just how these electrical patterns become the thoughts and sensations of the conscious mind remains a great and profound mystery. Nor do scientists fully understand the workings of the unconscious mind, those basic, instinctual emotions that seem to originate from deep within the brain's oldest and most primitive regions. Recent brain research has revealed that human beings have not one brain, but three. Differing from one another in structure and function, yet intimate-

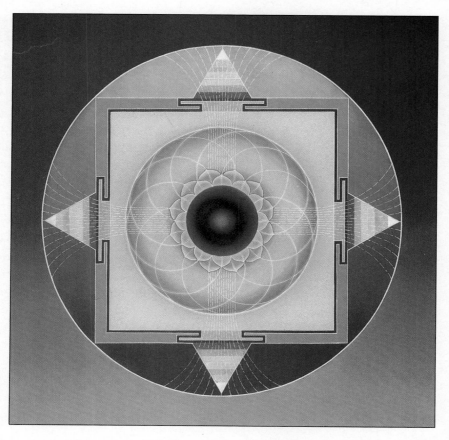

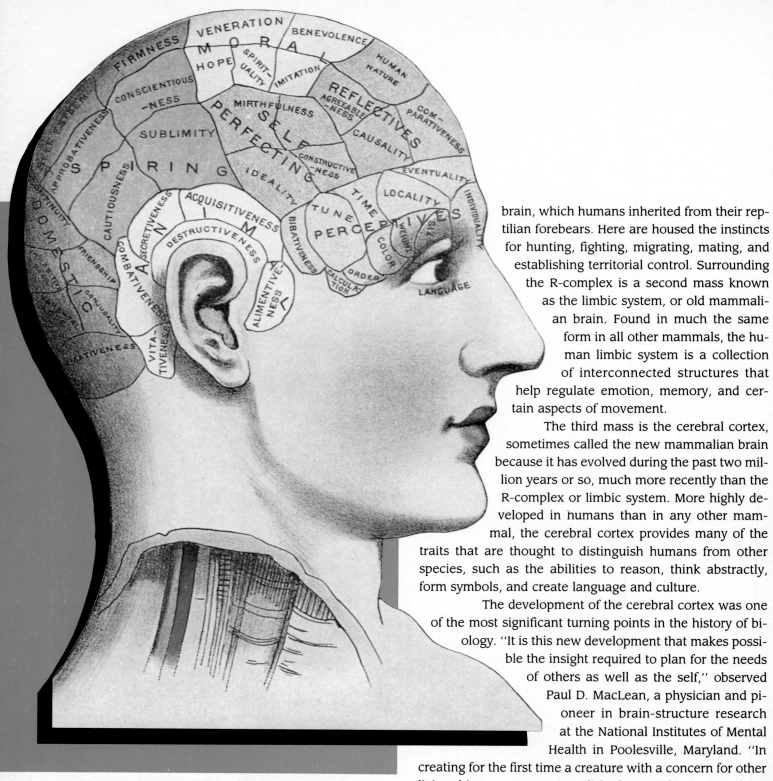

brain, which humans inherited from their reptilian forebears. Here are housed the instincts for hunting, fighting, migrating, mating, and establishing territorial control. Surrounding the R-complex is a second mass known as the limbic system, or old mammalian brain. Found in much the same form in all other mammals, the human limbic system is a collection of interconnected structures that help regulate emotion, memory, and certain aspects of movement.

The third mass is the cerebral cortex, sometimes called the new mammalian brain because it has evolved during the past two million years or so, much more recently than the R-complex or limbic system. More highly developed in humans than in any other mammal, the cerebral cortex provides many of the traits that are thought to distinguish humans from other species, such as the abilities to reason, think abstractly, form symbols, and create language and culture.

The development of the cerebral cortex was one of the most significant turning points in the history of biology. ''It is this new development that makes possible the insight required to plan for the needs of others as well as the self,'' observed Paul D. MacLean, a physician and pioneer in brain-structure research at the National Institutes of Mental Health in Poolesville, Maryland. ''In creating for the first time a creature with a concern for other living things, nature accomplished a 180-degree turnabout from what had previously been a reptile-eat-reptile and dog-eat-dog world.''

The discovery that the human brain has different regions with different functions has led to several structural explanations for the difference between the conscious and unconscious mind. British psychologist Stan Gooch offers

A 1923 phrenology chart links skull areas to attributes of character and intelligence. In the nineteenth century, even some scientists endorsed this system of reading bumps on the head.

ly interrelated, these three neural masses are believed to have become superimposed one on another during millions of years of evolution. The first, smallest, and most primitive of these masses is known as the R-complex, or reptilian

one such explanation in his 1972 book, *Total Man.* A human is a dual being, Gooch argues, consisting of a rational Ego—the part of the being that is considered the real self—and a darker, more intuitive, and less acknowledged Self. Gooch believes that the Ego is housed in the cerebral cortex, the more modern part of the brain; the Self inhabits a section of the older limbic system known as the cerebellum. The cerebellum regulates and coordinates muscular activity, and according to Gooch, it is also the seat of the unconscious. From that area of the brain, he says, come hypnagogic hallucinations—those frightening, dreamlike images that we occasionally experience in the state between waking and sleeping—and such sinister figures as vampires, troglodytes, and the devil.

Gooch also believes paranormal experiences arise from the cerebellum. In his 1978 book, *The Paranormal,* he describes how, at the age of twenty-six, he experienced a ''mediumistic trance.'' Gooch had accompanied a friend to a séance in Coventry. Soon after the séance began, Gooch felt inexplicably lightheaded. ''And then suddenly it seemed to me that a great wind was rushing through the room,'' he wrote. ''In my ears was the deafening sound of roaring waters. . . . As I felt myself swept away I became unconscious.'' Later, when he again became aware of his surroundings, Gooch was told that several spirits had spoken through him. Gooch understood at once what had happened; he felt, he later wrote, as if he had been possessed. It was a physical sensation, he added, as if the spirits had slipped on his body much as they would a suit of clothes.

In Gooch's opinion, the source of such mystical experiences resides deep within the older reaches of the brain. Other researchers contend, however, that the source of paranormal occurrences lies much closer to the brain's surface—in the right hemisphere of the cerebral cortex. Scientists now know that the two halves of the cerebral cortex, though mirror images of each other, serve very different functions. The left hemisphere, or left brain, controls the right half of the body in most people and is more adept

In this 1886 British cartoon, a smug phrenologist applies calipers to a boy's cranial contours to determine the lad's adult career. Although phrenology was debunked decades ago, the late-twentieth-century revival of occultism has seen some renewed interest in the practice.

Return to Eden: The Chimpanzees Speak

According to first-century Jewish historian Josephus, the animals in the Garden of Eden spoke freely with Adam and Eve. But after the sundering of paradise, mutual understanding between beast and human ceased. In recent decades, however, in several primate research laboratories across the United States, the lines of communication seem to have been reopened: Researchers say more than a dozen chimpanzees have learned to speak.

For eons, people believed that language was a unique product of the human mind, a sign of the special relationship between humankind and the Divine. When scientists began to question this assumption, they turned to the chimpanzee, the human species' closest kin in the animal kingdom.

Anatomical differences from humans prevent chimps from speaking aloud. Therefore, researchers chose visual modes of expression for their experiments. In 1966, University of Nevada psychologists adopted a chimp named Washoe. They taught her more than 130 words in American Sign Language (ASL), the silent parlance of the deaf.

The scientists say Washoe created new expressions with words from her vocabulary and also spoke to herself in ASL: "We have often seen Washoe moving stealthily to a forbidden part of the yard signing 'quiet' to herself, or running pell-mell for the potty chair signing 'hurry,' " they reported.

Other chimp language experiments flourished as well. Yet Herb Terrace, a Columbia University psychologist, was not convinced. He maintained that a chimp was not speaking unless it created unique sentences spontaneously, a feat he thought had not been demonstrated by scientific method.

After running his own experiment with a chimpanzee named Nim, to whom Terrace taught more than 200 ASL words, the psychologist decided that the chimp never created his own sentences but rather mimicked his teachers' cues—and that the chimps in all the experiments had mindlessly imitated their keepers. Other researchers disagreed, challenging Terrace with new evidence: Without any help from human beings whatsoever, Washoe taught more than fifty words in ASL to a young male chimp she adopted.

Although even the most articulate chimp used just 200 words—a fraction of a normal human's vocabulary—and communicated only simple ideas, the animals' "achievement is staggering," wrote a science editor in 1979. "Twenty years ago we thought all they could do was hoot." Their feats have defied the notion that the human mind is the sole domain of language.

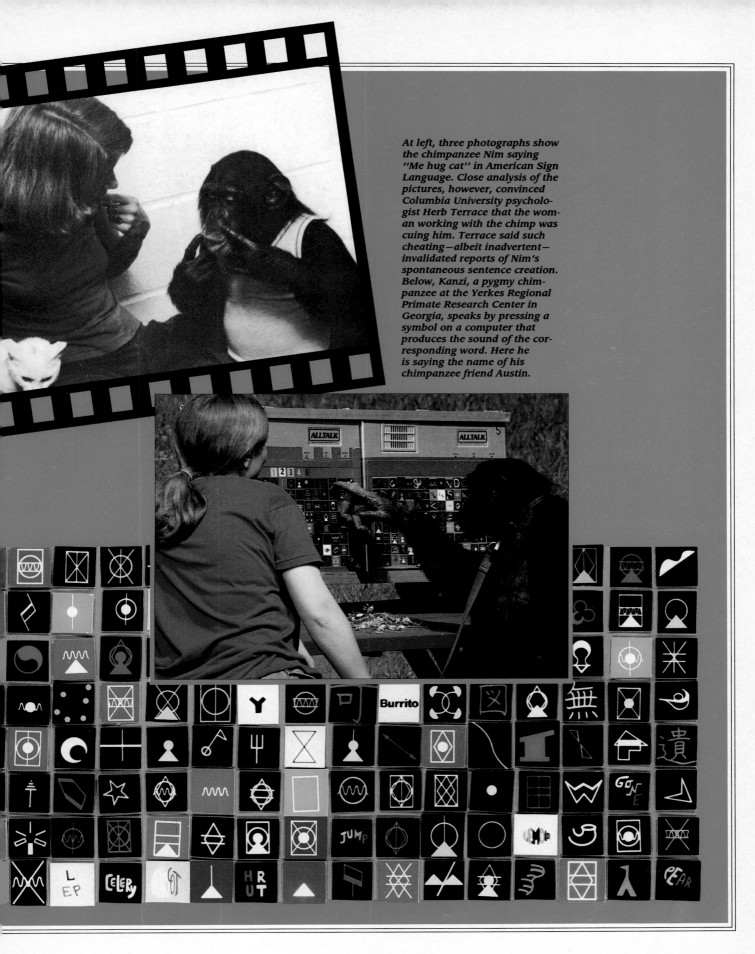

At left, three photographs show the chimpanzee Nim saying "Me hug cat" in American Sign Language. Close analysis of the pictures, however, convinced Columbia University psychologist Herb Terrace that the woman working with the chimp was cuing him. Terrace said such cheating—albeit inadvertent—invalidated reports of Nim's spontaneous sentence creation. Below, Kanzi, a pygmy chimpanzee at the Yerkes Regional Primate Research Center in Georgia, speaks by pressing a symbol on a computer that produces the sound of the corresponding word. Here he is saying the name of his chimpanzee friend Austin.

Example	Left hand	Right hand

With my right Hand

book

BOOK

"CUP"

Speech Center

Left Visual Field

These drawings reveal how operations that sever communication between the brain's hemispheres shed light on the functions of each half. At top, a right-handed split-brain patient approximated the examples successfully only with his left hand, because the right brain—which controls the left hand—handles spatial tasks. Below, a patient correctly pens the word book when it is presented to his left visual field. But when asked he says instead that he has written cup: The speech center in the left brain can only guess the activities of the left visual field, which is in the right brain.

at verbal reasoning, logical thinking, and deciphering abstract symbols such as numbers and words. The right brain controls the left half of the body and is more skilled at nonverbal, intuitive thought. And whereas the left hemisphere processes information in small, analytical steps, the right hemisphere looks at an entire situation all at once and responds accordingly. The right brain, therefore, is believed by many to be the source of both creativity and a certain cosmic wisdom—a higher and more intuitive form of knowledge and understanding.

One researcher who subscribes to that line of thinking is Julian Jaynes, a professor of psychology at Princeton University. Curiosity about why speech areas could be found in only one hemisphere of the human brain led Jaynes to develop a startling theory about human consciousness and mystical experiences. In his controversial 1976 book, *The Origins of Consciousness in the Breakdown of the Bicameral Mind,* Jaynes argued that as recently as 2000 BC, humans possessed no self-awareness, or inner life. As evidence, Jaynes pointed to the Greek poet Homer's *Iliad,* whose characters, he said, were incapable of self-reflection. "The characters of the *Iliad* do not sit down

and think out what to do. They have no conscious minds such as we say we have, and certainly no introspections," wrote Jaynes. Without self-awareness, he added, the characters also have no notion of free will, nor any sense of responsibility for their actions. Instead, it is the gods who intervene in their lives and make them do things. For example, when Achilles accuses Agamemnon of stealing his mistress, Agamemnon claims that the gods made him do it: "Not I was the cause, but Zeus and Destiny and Erinys that walketh in the darkness, who put into my soul fierce madness. . . . What could I do?"

From this observation, Jaynes developed the most controversial element of his theory: In the absence of self-consciousness, the godlike voices that the Greeks of the *Iliad* and other ancient humans heard and responded to were auditory hallucinations. Such hallucinations, Jaynes maintained, are still experienced by modern humans, but usually only during times of stress. Jaynes claims to have experienced a vivid auditory hallucination of his own. It occurred during his late twenties, at a time when he was living alone in Boston and struggling to work out the ideas that later became his theory of the bicameral—or divided—mind. "One afternoon," he wrote, "I lay down in intellectual despair on a couch. Suddenly, out of an absolute quiet, there came a firm, distinct loud voice from my upper right which said, 'Include the knower in the known!' It lugged me to my feet absurdly exclaiming, 'Hello?' looking for whoever was in the room. The voice had an exact location. No one was there!"

Jaynes believes these internal voices originate in the right hemisphere of the brain. "The language of men was involved with only one hemisphere in order to leave the other free for the language of gods," he deduced. Some of the vestiges of "godlike" ability still remain in the right hemisphere of the brain, according to Jaynes, and are expressed in such varied forms as artistic creativity, religious frenzy, and schizophrenia.

Although Hippocrates wrote of the possibility of the duality of the human brain as long ago as 400 BC, for many centuries the idea was largely ignored. The prevalent view was that the brain was a single, integrated organ. One scientist who thought differently was English physician Sir Thomas Browne, who, in 1684, after years of medical observation, proposed that the two hemispheres of the brain might control different types of behavior. In 1745, another physician reported the case of a male patient whose left brain had been badly damaged by a stroke. Because the only word the man spoke was "yes," he was forced to communicate by making signs with his hands. Yet despite this handicap, the report continued, the man could "sing certain hymns, which he had learned before he became ill, as clearly and distinctly as any healthy person." This phenomenon—the ability to sing but not to speak—has since been observed in many brain-damaged patients and is now recognized as one indication that singing and other musical abilities are a right-brain function.

By the mid-nineteenth century, reports of strange behaviors observed in other brain-damaged patients had convinced a small but growing number of scientists that the two brain halves had distinct, specialized functions. The evidence became compelling in April 1861 when French surgeon and neuroanatomist Pierre-Paul Broca made a startling presentation at a meeting of the Paris Anthropological Society. Broca told the story of a patient who, until the time of his death, had suffered from a severe difficulty in speaking known as aphasia. Friends had given the man the nick-

name Tan Tan because those were the only words he could utter. Yet, although the man's speech had been severely impaired, he had been able to understand what was said to him and to respond with facial expressions and hand gestures. Only his ability to speak had been restricted.

After telling the story of Tan Tan to the scientists gathered at the Paris meeting, Broca then revealed the exhibit he had brought with him. It was Tan Tan's brain. Pointing to a damaged area about the size of a hen's egg within the brain's left hemisphere, Broca proposed to the membership that this damage had been the cause of Tan Tan's speech problem.

It was a powerful presentation, and many scientists who heard it at the meeting or who read about it later became convinced that certain brain functions—in this case, language—did reside in specific areas of the brain. Other evidence soon followed. In 1874, German neurologist Carl Wernicke reported the discovery of a different type of aphasia caused by damage to another area of the brain's left hemisphere. Unlike Tan Tan, patients with what became known as Wernicke's aphasia had no trouble making verbal sounds. On the contrary, they were extremely verbose. Their impairment involved the inability to make their speech comprehensible to others; it simply came out sounding like gibberish.

Knowledge of the independence of the two brain hemispheres advanced dramatically after the development in the 1940s of a radical surgical procedure for severe and incurable epilepsy. The procedure involved severing the corpus callosum, the thick, pencil-shaped band of some 50 million nerve fibers that connects the right and left hemispheres of the brain and makes possible the transference of information from one hemisphere to the other. Before the development of this daring new surgical procedure, those epileptic patients with incurable seizures that did not respond to medication died from the extensive brain damage caused when the seizure crossed from one brain hemisphere to the other. Surgeons found that by cutting the cor-

P.B. inv.

pus callosum, they could restrict seizures to a single hemisphere, thus limiting the resultant damage to brain cells.

Not only was the surgery successful in treating that form of epilepsy, but much to the astonishment and relief of surgeons and patients alike, it also appeared to produce no noticeable change in personality, temperament, or intellectual abilities. One of these so-called split-brain patients, a twelve-year-old boy, was able upon awakening from the surgery to successfully repeat the tongue twister "Peter Piper picked a peck of pickled peppers." Another patient, a World War II veteran whose seizures had started when bomb shrapnel pierced his brain, claimed after the operation to feel better than he had in years. "In casual conversation over a cup of coffee and a cigarette, one would hardly suspect that there was anything at all unusual about him," remarked a neurosurgeon who interviewed the veteran after his surgery.

But subtle neurological changes had occurred, changes that became fully apparent only some twenty years later, when split-brain patients were given a more extensive battery of evaluative tests. Those specially designed tests were conducted at the California Institute of Technology under the guidance of psychobiologist Roger Sperry, who later won a Nobel Prize in physiology and medicine for his split-brain research. The procedures provided startling evidence that the operation had isolated the distinct functions of the brain's two hemispheres.

Sperry and one of his students, Michael Gazzaniga, began their tests on a forty-eight-year-old man nicknamed W. J., who had undergone a split-brain operation to cure his epilepsy. The scientists found that when a simple written instruction, such as "move your hand," was flashed to W. J.'s left visual field—which projects only to the right hemisphere of the brain—W. J. would not respond. Although his right brain had received the message, it could not comprehend its meaning and therefore could not instruct the hand to move. In another experiment, W. J. was given a standard set of red and white blocks to arrange in a picture design. His right hand—controlled by the left side of the brain—was unable to perform the task, but his left hand could do it quite easily. "The claim that we based on those findings," Gazzaniga later recalled, "was that the left hemisphere is dominant for language processes and the right hemisphere is dominant for visual-constructional tasks."

Through the study of W. J. and other split-brain patients, Sperry and Gazzaniga confirmed the remarkable independence of the two brain halves. The hemispheres were even found capable of working simultaneously on different tasks. Using a split-screen monitor, the doctors flashed the word *clap* to a patient's right brain and the word *laugh* to her left brain. She immediately laughed and clapped. But when asked, the woman said the only command she had seen on the screen was the one to laugh. Her right brain could not verbalize the command it had seen—to clap—but could carry it out, even at the same time the left brain was obeying its command to laugh.

This kind of results have led to speculation that within each individual there may exist two separate selves, or personalities, one residing in the brain's left hemisphere, the other in the right. In fact, Gazzaniga has concluded that each hemisphere has its own memories, values, and emotions. At times, he says, they may not agree with each other. For example, when Gazzaniga asked the right hemisphere of a young split-brain patient called Paul what he wanted to be, the answer came back "an automobile racer." But when he asked the same question of Paul's left hemisphere, the answer was "a draftsman." Paul was also periodically given a multiple-choice test in which he was asked to rate some of his interests on a one-to-five scale, from "like very much" to "dislike very much." The test was administered separately to his right and left brains. One day, the answers from the two brains were diametrically opposite each other. Whatever one hemisphere liked, the other disliked. Paul himself was in a very bad temper that day, verbally abusive and argumentative. A month later, on a day when he exhibited a calm and pleasant mood, he took the test again. This time his two hemispheres rated all the items on the test the

Aided by attendants, two women suffering from epilepsy stumble to a healing site in this 1642 engraving. When the group reaches a certain bridge, the men will force their charges to dance to bagpipe music, an exercise that was once believed to purge epileptics of seizures.

Mental Workouts That May Be Worthless—or Worse

"I spend way too much time on my triceps and not enough on my concepts," confessed a client at the Visconti 2000 Mind/Brain Fitness Center in Cambridge, Massachusetts. Like hundreds of others, he resolved to start toning his mind on trendy equipment such as the Synchro-Energizer *(below, right)*.

This brainier cousin of weightlifting machines is a futuristic-looking headpiece with goggles that flash colored lights and headphones that pulse musical tones. Benefits of its audiovisual bombardment reportedly include a balancing of the two hemispheres of the brain that enthusiasts say can relieve stress, end problems with substance abuse, and boost creativity, self-esteem, and even IQ.

The Synchro-Energizer is but one of many such machines. Another, the Lumitron, operates on theories about the psychological effects of color. Mind trainers program its TV screen—mounted inside a canvas hood worn over the head—to display any color of the spectrum deemed appropriate for the client. Red, for instance, allegedly stimulates the brain, while violet is thought to relax it.

The Graham Potentializer—a bed that rotates in a magnetic field to the sound of relaxing music—supposedly soothes an anxiety-ridden client by rocking the fluids of the inner ear. The motion is said to prepare the mind not only for visualization of the accomplishment of goals but even for so-called out-of-body experiences.

Critics note that no controlled experiments have proved the efficacy of any of these machines, which some call the snake oil of the electronic era. In fact, a flashing light such as that projected by the Synchro-Energizer can be dangerous: It may induce epileptic seizures in people susceptible to them.

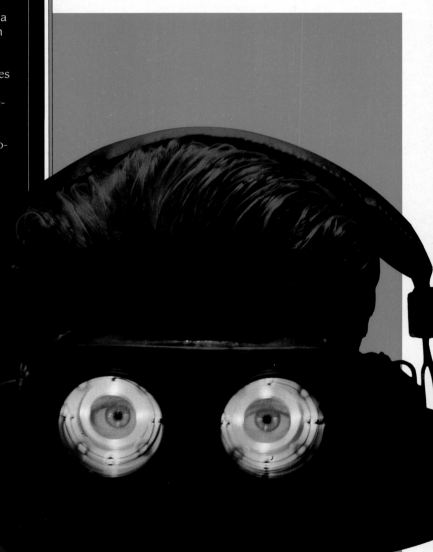

same. Gazzaniga concluded that the human brain is constantly involved in this type of warring and that dissonance between the two hemispheres may be a very simple cause of anxiety and tension.

Paul's was an extremely unusual case. Whereas the right hemisphere of most split-brain patients is completely mute, his became capable of some language communication. Yet his left hemisphere always remained the dominant of the two and would sometimes use its much superior language skills to rationalize the

Two Italians match wits over a chess game as friends look on in this 1493 woodcut. Thought to have originated in seventh-century India, chess has long been touted as a mind-sharpening exercise.

ease to a specific area of either the right or left hemisphere. For example, few split-brain patients experience trouble speaking after their surgery, for although the left brain has been severed from the right, it has not experienced any direct damage. But, as Paul Broca and Carl Wernicke discovered more than a century ago, direct damage to one of the main speech centers in the left hemisphere will leave an individual either unable to speak or unable to produce meaningful speech. Damage to other areas of the left brain can cause

puzzling actions performed by the right hemisphere. In one test, a picture of a chicken's claw was shown to Paul's left brain while a picture of a snow scene was shown simultaneously to his right. Then he was asked to look at a series of other pictures and choose a shot that corresponded to the one he had just seen. With his right hand, Paul chose a picture of a chicken, and with his left hand he selected a picture of a snow shovel. Paul explained his choices by remarking, ''The chicken claw goes with the chicken, and you need a shovel to clean out the chicken's shed.'' This, of course, was Paul's left hemisphere talking. His right hemisphere could not speak for itself and explain why it had chosen the snow shovel, so his left hemisphere, which had no knowledge of the snow-scene picture, constructed as plausible an explanation as it could.

The behavioral anomalies of people who have undergone split-brain surgery are usually quite different from those who have experienced damage through injury or dis-

such specific disorders as name amnesia, an inability to recall names of familiar people, or word deafness, a condition in which a person can read, write, and speak normally but is unable to comprehend spoken words.

One of the most famous cases of left-brain damage involved the great French composer Maurice Ravel. As a result of a tumor that damaged his brain's left hemisphere, Ravel suffered from a severe form of Wernicke's aphasia. Although he continued to listen to and enjoy music, he was unable to read music or play the piano again. Most frustrating of all, however, was his inability to write down the cascade of musical notes he heard in his head. From 1926 until his death, at age sixty-two, following a 1937 brain operation, Ravel never composed again.

Injuries to the right hemisphere of the brain disrupt visual perception and spatial orientation rather than language skills. Many right-brain-damaged people, for exam-

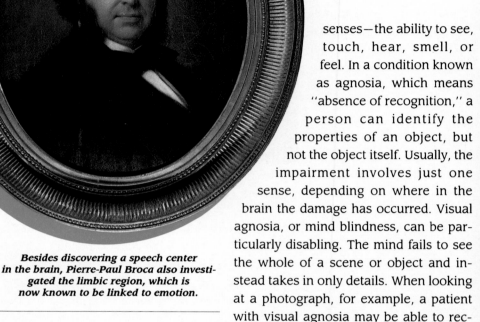

Besides discovering a speech center in the brain, Pierre-Paul Broca also investigated the limbic region, which is now known to be linked to emotion.

ple, have difficulty putting together simple jigsaw puzzles or following directions on a map. They also become disoriented easily and may wander about lost in familiar places, including their own homes. Musicians whose right brains are injured often forget how to play their instruments or how to sing, a condition known as amusia.

Perhaps one of the most bizarre, and rare, conditions caused by damage to the brain's right hemisphere is neglect syndrome, a neurological disorder that leaves people behaving as if the left side of their visual perception—and even the left side of their bodies—no longer exists. A man with this disorder may shave only the right side of his face, or a woman may apply lipstick to only the right half of her lips. When asked to copy a picture of a house or a clock, people with neglect syndrome draw only the right-hand side of the object—and think nothing is amiss. Sometimes, such patients can have a complete loss of awareness of their left arms or legs and in extreme cases may not even acknowledge that the limbs belong to them. Oliver Sacks wrote of one such man whom he encountered lying on the floor in a hospital ward. The man claimed that someone had tried to play a horrific joke on him by attaching a severed leg to his body. No matter how hard he tried, said the frightened man, he could not tear the disgusting limb from his flesh. Sacks calmed the patient, gently explaining that the leg belonged to the man and not to a cadaver. The patient was not easily convinced, however. Sacks then asked him where he thought his left leg was, if the leg he was trying to remove was not it. "I don't know," said the man. "I have no idea. It's disappeared. It's gone. It's nowhere to be found."

Other damage to the brain specifically affects the senses—the ability to see, touch, hear, smell, or feel. In a condition known as agnosia, which means "absence of recognition," a person can identify the properties of an object, but not the object itself. Usually, the impairment involves just one sense, depending on where in the brain the damage has occurred. Visual agnosia, or mind blindness, can be particularly disabling. The mind fails to see the whole of a scene or object and instead takes in only details. When looking at a photograph, for example, a patient with visual agnosia may be able to recognize an automobile or a building or a person walking but will not be able to put these elements together to recognize that it is a photograph of a city street. To identify what they cannot recognize by sight alone, people with visual agnosia must use their other senses. When one man with very severe visual agnosia was shown a rose, he could not identify it at all. When he was permitted to touch it, he described it abstractly as "a convoluted red form with a linear green attachment." Only when he was told to smell the flower did he guess its true identity.

The specific inability to recognize faces, even one's own, is known as prosopagnosia. This form of agnosia seems to arise from damage to the right side of the occipital lobe, the visual center of the brain located at the rear of the cerebral cortex. Because the area of the brain responsible for voice recognition is on the opposite side of the brain, a person with prosopagnosia usually can place the faces of friends and relatives as soon as they start to speak. In some instances, patients lose not only the ability to recognize faces but the very idea of a "face."

Damage to the brain can cause even broader concepts

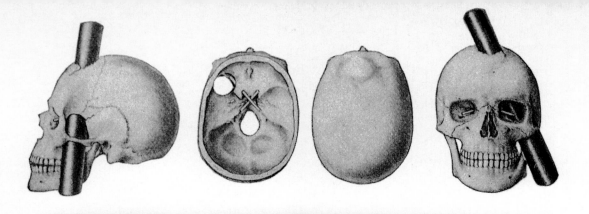

to be lost to the mind. In one highly unusual case reported by Oliver Sacks, a stroke patient suffered such extensive damage to the occipital lobe that he became completely blind—but did not know it. "He had lost all visual images and memories, lost them totally—yet had no sense of any loss," wrote Sacks. "Indeed, he had lost the very idea of seeing—and was not only unable to describe anything visually, but was bewildered when I used words such as 'seeing' and 'light.' He had become, in essence, a nonvisual being."

Drawings re-create the dramatic head injury sustained in 1848 by Phineas Gage. Remarkably, he recovered fully, or so it seemed until his friends recognized that he was "no longer Gage." From this incident, scientists learned that damage to the frontal cortex affects personality.

Author of the book that inspired the 1990 film Awakenings, New York neurologist Oliver Sacks exudes a sober compassion in this photograph. His chronicles brought the mysterious world of brain disorders to public attention.

In rare and tragic cases involving neurological damage, people lose a form of sensation scientists have named proprioception, which is the awareness of the physical body. From the Latin meaning "received from self," proprioception is the hidden sense that enables the mind to be aware of the location and movement of the body's muscles and limbs. It works with great precision and with very little conscious effort. The decision to clap one's hands, for example, takes a moment of conscious thought, but once the decision has been made, the body carries forth the order without much self-awareness. It can even be done with the eyes shut—all because of proprioception.

For a person who has lost this sense, clapping two hands together takes extreme concentration and effort. Without a sense of where the body is in space, putting two hands together becomes an almost impossible task. The person is not paralyzed—the muscles are still capable of movement—but *disembodied*. Patients without proprioception feel as if they have "lost" their arms or legs. "I think they're one place, and I find they're another," noted one woman who developed the condition at age twenty-seven. "It's like the body's blind."

The woman eventually learned to move again by using her vision to compensate for the loss of proprioception. She spent hour after hour monitoring her movements, watching each part of her body carefully as it moved. She learned how to stand erect, walk, hold a knife and fork, even type at a computer—in short, to do all the simple, unpremeditated movements of everyday life. Yet for her, such movements were no longer natural and effortless but required an immense and conscious effort. Everything had to be done by vision, not feel. If she let her concentration slip for even a second, she would collapse onto the floor.

Damage to the brain does not always have a debilitating outcome, however. Occasionally a physiological change will occur in the brain that enhances the senses or that unleashes a hidden sensory potential of which most humans are not normally aware. Indeed, some scientists believe that many phenomena often attributed to a sixth sense—such as telepathy and clairvoyance—are really the result of one or more of the five standard senses going haywire and functioning in a supernormal way. For example, in the rare brain disorder called synesthesia, discovered more than two centuries ago, the senses are joined in a mysterious way that enables people to actually see sounds, feel flavors, and taste colors or words. To a synesthete, the sound of a telephone ringing may look like diamond-shaped blocks, or the word *telephone* may taste like apple pie. The most common form of synesthesia is called *audition colorée,* or "colored hearing." "One of the things I love about my husband," noted one synesthete, "are the colors of his voice and his laugh. It's a wonderful golden brown, with a flavor of crisp, buttery toast, which sounds very odd, I know, but it is very real."

Intrigued by such perplexing comments, Washington, D.C., neurologist Richard Cytowic monitored the brains of synesthetic people as they were actually experiencing colored sounds and discovered an unusual pattern of blood flow. Normally, blood flow increases in the cerebral cortex during sensory stimulation. Cytowic found, however, that when a person is "seeing" sounds, blood flow decreases in the cerebral cortex and increases in the deeper and more primitive limbic system. "The brain's higher information processing turns off during colored hearing," Cytowic said. "An older, more fundamental way of viewing the world—more mammalian than language-related—takes over." According to Cytowic and other researchers who have studied the phenomenon, many ordinary people continue to exhibit rudimentary remnants of synesthesia. For example, they experience lower and higher musical tones as having different colorations and see the various days of the week as having different colors.

A variation of synesthesia is the condition known as "skin vision," or eyeless sight. Although this strange phenomenon was first reported in the 1920s by the French novelist and physician Jules Romains, scientists did not begin to take it seriously until 1962—when a young Russian woman named Rosa Kuleshova first astonished members of Moscow's Biophysics Institute of the Soviet Academy of Sciences by her apparent ability to read printed words and distinguish colors with her fingers. Kuleshova told the scientists that the ability had developed gradually, beginning with the third and fourth fingers of her right hand, then spreading to all her fingers, eventually reaching her elbow and other body parts as well.

When the news of Kuleshova's seemingly psychic ability was made public, she became an overnight sensation. The young woman was invited to demonstrate her talents on stage. She was overwhelmed by the sudden attention, however, and soon began making extravagant claims that she could fulfill only by cheating. Despite her transgressions, researchers of the phenomenon believed Kuleshova's abilities were genuine and with further investigation discovered that they were not unique. A Soviet professor named Abram Novomeysky reported that of the persons he tested, one in six of those could learn within half an hour to differentiate between two colors by touch. Like Kuleshova, some subjects eventually learned to identify all primary colors by their feel. Most of those tested agreed on how the different colors "felt." They said that yellow, for example, was slippery, and that orange was hard and rough. Some subjects honed their skills to such a degree that they no longer needed to touch the colors. They explained that since each hue radiated its particular texture to a different height, it was possible to identify a color by merely passing a hand over it. Red appeared to radiate highest and light blue lowest. From this research, Novomeysky came to believe that skin vision was the result of an interaction between electromagnetic fields emanating both from the "reader's" fingertips and from the color being read.

Just as some people display remarkable sensory abilities, such as skin vision or colored hearing, others have an extraordinary capacity for memory. The nineteenth-century English historian Thomas Macaulay was said to have such a remarkable memory that he could quote a chapter of a book verbatim after reading it only once. To win a wager, he once memorized John Milton's epic *Paradise Lost* in a single night. Also credited with incredible mnemonic powers was the Yugoslav-born American inventor Nikola Tesla. He never wrote mathematical problems down on paper but instead worked them out entirely in his head. Tesla was also able to "see" his inventions in his mind long before he sketched blueprints for them. These mental images were so precise and detailed that they included dimensions down to ten-thousandths of an inch.

The design for a new machine sometimes popped into Tesla's mind quite unexpectedly. Such was the case with his most famous invention, the alternating-current generator, a device that ushered in the age of electricity. One evening in 1882, while walking with a companion in a park in Prague, Tesla apparently fell into a sudden trancelike state. His body swayed slowly from side to side; his arms flailed the air. Then he saw it: a clear and detailed vision of an alternating-current motor, a machine unknown at that time. "The idea came like a flash of lightning, and in an instant the truth was revealed," Tesla recalled later. "The images I saw were wonderfully sharp and clear and had the solidity of metal and stone, so much so that I told him [the friend], 'See my motor here; watch me reverse it.' I cannot describe my emotions. Pygmalion seeing his statue come to life could not have been more deeply moved." Despite his excitement, Tesla did not rush back to his laboratory to make a rough sketch of his new invention. He knew the machine's image would remain etched in his memory indefinitely. Indeed, a year later, when Tesla was finally ready to make a working model of the generator, the image was as sharp and clear in his mind as it had been the day he had first envisioned it.

Both Macaulay and Tesla had eidetic, or photographic, memory, the ability to summon up visual images with ex-

traordinary accuracy. Many young children possess this type of memory, as evidenced by their ability to describe drawings from their favorite storybooks in minute detail. For reasons that remain unknown, however, the power is rarely retained past puberty. Some scientists believe that the brain becomes more selective as it matures; rather than remembering an entire drawing from a book, the adult brain remembers only the most relevant images and then tosses out the rest.

Eidetic memory appears to be literally limitless. As reported in the 1990 edition of the *Guinness Book of World Records,* in 1967, one Mehmed Ali Halici of Turkey recited from memory 6,666 verses of the Koran in six hours. And in 1989, Englishman Tony Power memorized in correct order a random sequence of thirteen packs of shuffled playing cards—676 cards in all—after looking at them only once. But the world record for a single eidetic memory feat may be held by Bhandanta Vicitasara of Rangoon, Burma, who in 1974 correctly recited from memory 16,000 pages of Buddhist canonical texts.

These feats notwithstanding, the most celebrated case of a mnemonist, or "person with a vast and endless memory," is that of a man known simply as S., a patient of the great Soviet psychologist Aleksandr Luria. In the early 1920s, the young S., a reporter for a Moscow paper, went to see Luria at the suggestion of his editor. The editor had been astounded by S.'s memory skills—at his ability, for example, to remember long lists of addresses and detailed assignment instructions without taking notes. Luria, who had always been fascinated by memory and its capabilities, immediately tested S. by asking him to repeat several random series of words and numbers. The reporter complied with ease. Luria increased the number of elements in the series from thirty to fifty, and then to seventy. He presented them to S. in writing as well as orally. But the reporter's performance remained steadfast; he never made an error.

"As the experimenter, I soon found myself in a state verging on utter confusion," Luria wrote of this first meeting with S. "An increase in the length of a series led to no

The Senses: Bringing the World Inside

Gateways to consciousness, the senses gather information from external reality and relay it to the brain. They supply the mind with food for thought, and all awareness depends upon their input.

Most human beings possess smell, touch, taste, hearing, and vision, but people lacking one or more of these compensate by sharpening their remaining senses or even by developing new ones. The blind, for instance, often maneuver by a kind of sonar system resembling that of such dwellers in darkness as bats, pit vipers, and whales. They discriminate among objects by reading their different echoes.

Helen Keller, both blind and deaf, cultivated intense awareness of smell, touch, and taste. She could discern people's professions simply by their odor, and she distinguished cornets from strings in a symphony broadcast over the radio by feeling the vibrations from the box with her hands.

Scientists have learned that consciousness receives only a fraction of the data collected by the senses because a filtering system protects the mind from sensory overload. Yet this mechanism also limits perception of reality. An Australian physicist likens this restricted world-view to being "a prisoner in a tower permitted to look through five slits at the landscape outside." These slits widen, however, for those under the influence of drugs or in the throes of disease. People suffering from a pituitary disorder called Addison's disease, for example, are 150 times more sensitive to taste than are healthy people.

Some people, such as successful dowsers or reputed psychics, supposedly draw upon an unexplained mode of perception—a sixth sense. Researchers have found that many of these apparent miracle workers suffered brain damage earlier in life. The trauma may have disturbed the mind's sensory filter system, purportedly allowing a host of paranormal experiences to enter consciousness.

SMELL

Brains evolved over the eons from olfactory stalks; thus the earliest creatures could smell before they could think. Today the ancient sense of smell wields a subtle power, enhancing survival of the species by facilitating the sexual response that certain scents trigger. For example, girls who live among men—and hence smell them—reach puberty sooner than those who do not. Similarly, a male sexually involved with a woman grows facial hair faster than one who is not, because the female odor encourages the production of testosterone.

TOUCH

Experiencing touch is vital to development. In a study on premature infants in hospital incubators, an experimental group was physically stimulated through gentle massage while a control group was not. The massaged babies gained weight 47 percent faster than those who were not touched. Furthermore, their nervous systems matured faster and they were discharged from the hospital an average of six days earlier. Experiments with baby monkeys show that those who experience even slight deprivation of touch suffer actual brain damage.

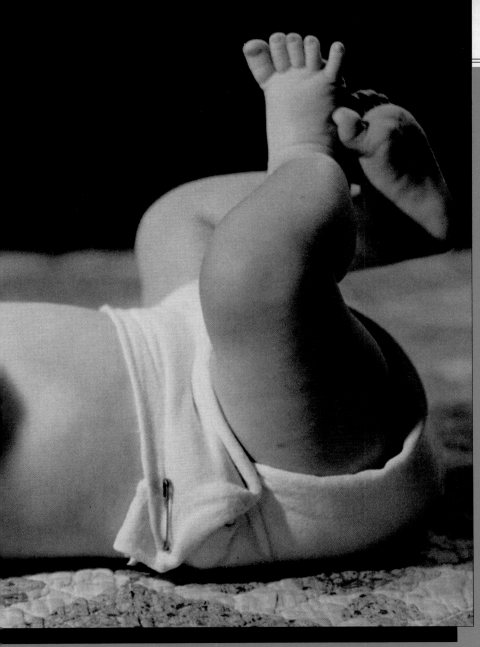

A mirthful baby clasps its hands in this photograph snapped during the first few months of life. Infants dwell almost exclusively in the realm of the senses, dependent upon ample stimulation of all five for timely development and good health.

TASTE

At the start of French novelist Marcel Proust's largely autobiographical book *Swann's Way,* the main character mingles in his mouth a sip of tea and a few morsels of a small shell-shaped cake called a madeleine. So evocative is the sense of taste that this simple act recalls for him an entire era of his childhood. Ten thousand buds dotting the inside of the mouth equip humans with the ability to taste substances sweet, salty, sour, and bitter. All other flavors are actually odors: An air shaft connecting the mouth and nose links the olfactory and gustatory senses.

HEARING

The ability to hear inspires in human beings a panoply of emotions, ranging from the fury induced by the throbbing drums in a macumba ritual to the reflective calm evoked by repeating the Indian mantra ''om.'' From the moment of conception, a fetus grows in comfort hearing the reassuring regularity of its mother's heartbeat. Doctors use music to stimulate comatose patients and to draw out autistic children. And when human beings hear their own voices raised in song, their levels of endorphins—feel-good chemicals in the brain—rise.

SIGHT

A tireless seeker of beauty, the eye has guided much of cultural development since humans first walked the earth. In order to meet the sight organ's rigorous standards, people have long sought to make the world—and themselves—more lovely to behold. Women of Renaissance Italy and Victorian England, for instance, dropped the juice of the poisonous belladonna plant into their eyes to dilate their pupils. And some modern men and women endure endless exercise workouts and even undergo surgery in the quest for an eye-pleasing body.

Inventor Nikola Tesla studies before an electric generator that his extraordinary memory allowed him to plan out entirely in his mind. "Without ever having drawn a sketch," he explained in 1921, "I can give the measurements of all parts, and all will fit."

noticeable increase in difficulty for S., and I simply had to admit that the capacity of his memory had no distinct limits; that I had been unable to perform what one would think was the simplest task a psychologist can do: measure the capacity of an individual's memory."

Intrigued, Luria asked S. to return for more tests. Thus began a professional relationship that would last for thirty years. In 1968, Luria published the results of his experiments with the Moscow reporter in a now classic book, *The Mind of a Mnemonist.*

Luria learned that S. not only had far better recall than most people but that he also underwent the process of memorizing in a unique way. Because he could see clearly in his mind the numbers or words he memorized, S. merely called up the sequence he wanted and then read it back. It made little difference whether he was asked to "read" the sequence from beginning to end or end to beginning, or to skip about in some fashion and recite, say, every third item.

As Luria discovered, when S. reeled off a sequence of words or numbers, he was seeing in his mind not the actual symbols that create the words or numbers but distinctive forms. S.'s memory was based on synesthesia; he saw colored splotches, lines, and other patterns when he heard sounds or when he looked at numbers. "For me 2, 4, 6, 5 are not just numbers," S. wrote in his journal. "They have forms." The number 2, he said, is flat and rectangular and tinted a whitish gray; the number 5 is "absolutely complete and takes the form of a cone or a tower—something substantial." Just as educators have discovered in recent years that children learn best when all their senses are involved, so Luria found that S.'s synesthetic skills enhanced his memorization. "I recognize a word not only by the images it evokes but by a whole complex of feelings that image arouses," S. told Luria. "It's hard to express. . . . It's not a matter of vision or hearing but some overall sense I get. Usually I experience a word taste and weight, and I don't have to make an effort to remember it—the word seems to recall itself. But it's difficult to describe. What I sense is

something oily slipping through my hand . . . or I'm aware of a slight tickling in my left hand caused by a mass of tiny, lightweight points. When that happens I simply remember, without having to make the attempt."

Because sounds and words became fused with images, both conversation and reading were difficult for S. "Even when I read about circumstances that are entirely new to me, if there happens to be a description, say, of a staircase, it turns out to be the one in a house I once lived in," he lamented. "I start to follow it and lose the gist of what I am reading." With his mind cluttered with so many erroneous details, S. found it difficult to lead a normal life. Although he married and had a child, his relationship with his family was a distant one, perceived through a haze by a mind burdened with endless images. He tried many different jobs, from stock-market analyst to vaudeville actor, but each seemed to present obstacles with which he could not cope. Eventually he became a professional "memory man," earning his living astounding audiences with his unparalleled feats of recall. Emotionally, it was a difficult, isolated life. As Luria wrote, "An individual whose conscious awareness is such that a sound becomes fused with a sense of color and taste; for whom each fleeting impression engenders a vivid, inextinguishable image; for whom words have quite different meanings than they do for us—such a person cannot mature in the same way others do, nor will his inner world, his life history tend to be like others."

Centuries ago, the ability to memorize prodigious amounts of information was considered an art tinged with magic. Ancient Greeks and Romans believed that calling upon past knowledge was a way of transcending one's immediate surroundings and, thus, of reaching a higher consciousness, a more intense reality. The memorization of great written works was seen as the key to wisdom as well as to knowledge, and as a renewable source of creative inspiration. Indeed, the Greeks made the goddess of memory, Mnemosyne, the mother of the nine Muses.

One of the most ardent practitioners of the art of memory was Giulio Camillo, a sixteenth-century Italian pro-

essor who spent much of his life designing a "memory the-ater." Camillo was quite famous in his day, and his theater, though never completed, was considered one of the great wonders of the world. The theater was circular, with a small central stage surrounded by seven tiers. The tiers were divided by aisles to form seven sections, representing Solomon's seven pillars of wisdom and the seven planets then known to astronomers. Each section had numerous exhibits of paintings, statues, or other objects meant to symbolize all of human knowledge. Under the exhibits were drawers containing various speeches based on Cicero, the unsurpassed orator of ancient Rome. Explaining the purpose behind his theater, Camillo observed, "it is right that we, wishing to store up eternally the eternal nature of all things which can be expressed in speech . . . should assign them to eternal places." Visitors were encouraged to spend time at each exhibit, to absorb the wisdom represented there and thus achieve a deeper and more meaningful sense of reality. It was Camillo's hope that the theater would "keep the mind awake and move the memory," enabling each visitor to perceive with his eyes everything that is otherwise hidden in the depths of the human mind."

Camillo was not the only scholar of his day to believe that memory possessed magical powers. Italian philosopher and cosmologist Giordano Bruno was convinced that the human mind was divine and contained within it the secrets of the heavens. If human beings could only discover this treasure, using the magical art of memory, he wrote in his 1582 book *The Art of Memory,* they would have at their fingertips all the forces of the cosmos.

The magical powers of the memory still elude most people today, including those researchers who are trying to find and map the source of the human memory and understand its capabilities. One of the first scientists to embark on that quest was the American neuropsychologist Karl Lashley. Starting in the 1920s, Lashley conducted a series of experiments on laboratory rats in which he systematically removed different areas of the animals' brains in an attempt

Ancient Tricks for Storing Thoughts

In the premodern world, where paper was scarce and such conveniences as computer disks and tape recorders unheard of, a sound memory was vital to success. Thus, people intent upon leaving their mark toiled diligently to expand their minds' storage bins of information, striving to catch evanescent thoughts before they plummeted into oblivion.

In classical Greece and Rome, memory was so highly valued that it was called an art. The earliest remaining treatise on it, penned by an anonymous first-century-BC Roman, described a complex mnemonic, or memory-assisting, strategy that involved crafting in the mind a warehouse for personal symbols.

The first step in this process, according to the writer, was to visualize a familiar place, preferably a large house or a spacious public building with plentiful

NEGATIO AFFIRMATIO N·R·S

GRAMATICA·

nooks and crannies. This served as the mental home for ideas to be memorized. The next task was to devise a symbol for each idea—something unusual or jarring enough to stick in the memory. These symbols were then placed in proper order in succeeding rooms in the house. To recall the entire group of thoughts, one visualized walking through the house and converting each symbol into the idea it signified.

Despite the fact that many people considered this method cumbersome and more likely to thwart than nurture memory, several writers echoed the nameless Roman during both the classical period and the Renaissance. In the sixteenth century, a German monk named Johannes Romberch wrote a similar scheme of recall in which the symbols for ideas were linked not to a single edifice but rather to a group, as illustrated at left above. The various buildings of an abbey became repositories for memory-jogging signs. Romberch also used as a mnemonic device a human figure thematically related to the subject to be memorized. In the drawing above, Gramatica, the personification of grammar, stands amid words and symbols intended to trigger recall of grammatical rules.

to pinpoint exactly where among the elaborately interlaced neurons memory is stored. In 1950, Lashley published a paper titled "In Search of the Engram," in which he reluctantly concluded that memory and learning are not centered in any one area of the brain but are instead diffused throughout it.

At the same time Lashley was admitting that memory could not be localized within the brain, another researcher, Canadian neurosurgeon Wilder Penfield, witnessed some strange events that seemed to indicate it could. To find the tiny scarred areas of the brain where epileptic seizures originate, Penfield had devised a procedure in which he could painlessly stimulate specific surface areas of the cerebral cortex with a small electrical probe. Because the patients remained conscious throughout the procedure, they could describe any sensations they experienced.

Quite unexpectedly, Penfield discovered that his probe could stimulate extremely detailed and often quite emotional memories when it touched areas of the temporal cortex, the portion of the cerebral cortex directly connected to the limbic system. The patients seemed to vividly relive the sights, sounds, tastes, and emotions of long-forgotten experiences. "Oh, gosh," exclaimed one twelve-year-old boy. "There they are, my brother is there. He is aiming an air rifle at me." Observed a young woman of her experience with the probe, "I had the same very, very familiar memory, in an office somewhere. I was there and someone was calling to me, a man leaning on the desk with a pencil in his hand." Other patients heard specific pieces of music, which they could hum note for note. One man was transported back to the South African farm where he used to live.

From his research, Penfield concluded that the brain records every sensation, every emotion, every experience of life yet offers only limited access to that immense store of information. Forgetting, therefore, is not the loss of memories but the inability to locate them. Penfield also concluded that the temporal cortex contained at least some of the neurons directly involved with memory. Scientists now believe, however, that although Penfield was placing his probe on the surface of the temporal cortex, it was really the underlying limbic system that the neurosurgeon was stimulating. More recent research has shown that several structures within this ancient part of the brain play a crucial role in memory formation.

One of those structures is the thalamus, a pea-size area at the center of the brain that serves as a relay station for almost all information coming into the brain. Damage to nerve cells within the thalamus has been directly linked to Korsakoff's syndrome, a memory disorder named for the Russian doctor who first described its symptoms in 1887. People with this disorder, which is usually caused by chronic alcoholism, have no recent memory and sometimes experience what is called retrograde amnesia, in which long stretches of memory may be obliterated. Victims of Korsakoff's syndrome can typically recall events in their distant past, but new memories cannot be established, nor can any new information be learned.

In *The Man Who Mistook His Wife for a Hat,* Oliver Sacks wrote about a forty-nine-year-old man he encountered in 1975. Jimmie, an affable ex-navy officer from Connecticut, had lost thirty years of memory to Korsakoff's syndrome. For Jimmie, it was always 1945 and he was perpetually nineteen years old. Anything new said or shown to him was forgotten within a few seconds' time. "He is," Sacks noted, "isolated in a single moment of being, with a moat or lacuna of forgetting all round him. . . . He is a man without a past (or future), stuck in a constantly changing, meaningless moment."

In another tragic case, a man known in medical literature simply by the initials H. M. led neuroscientists to implicate another structure of the limbic system—the hippocampus—in memory formation. One of the most ancient parts of the brain, the hippocampus is an inch-long curved section of gray matter located within the temporal cortex. In 1953, H. M. underwent a specialized form of brain surgery, devised just for him, to relieve the severe and life-threatening epileptic seizures he was experiencing almost daily. The surgeons intended to remove only H. M.'s temporal lobes, but they inadvertently removed part of his hippocampus as well.

Soon after the operation, H. M.'s doctors realized something had gone terribly wrong. Although his seizures had stopped, H. M. was unable to remember the names or even the faces of the nurses caring for him. If he left his room to walk down the hall, he could not remember how to return. When given a magazine, he would read the same article over and over without realizing he had read it before. His memory was fine for events that had happened prior to his operation, but he could not learn anything new. Like patients with Korsakoff's syndrome, H. M. had lost his ability to remember. He was a man forever stuck in the distant past and instantaneous present.

In many ways mentally retarded, but displaying uncanny pockets of genius, bespectacled twins Charles (left) and George ponder a math problem in 1966. Asked how they could remember so much information—300-figure digits, for example—they said, "We see it."

Whereas H. M. had consciousness without memory, people with savant syndrome—such as the twins, George and Charles, who were described earlier—have memory without consciousness. Savants are renowned for their exceptional eidetic memory in their particular island of talent—the twins' ability to describe the weather conditions of any past day in their lives, for example. The memory of savants, however, is automatic and habitual; it shows absolutely no sign of self-reflection, no cognitive awareness, and little emotional involvement.

Nevertheless, savants display quite extraordinary gifts. Alonzo Clemens, who suffered brain injury after a fall at age three, has an estimated IQ of forty. He can barely count to ten, and his vocabulary is limited to several hundred words—similar to that of a two-year-old child. Yet when handed a lump of clay, he can mold it into a magnificently detailed horse, dog, or other animal, with every muscle and tendon of the animal painstakingly revealed. His pieces are collected by art connoisseurs around the world, fetching prices as high as $45,000. Similarly, an autistic sixteen-year-old boy named Steven Wilcher has dazzled all of his native England with his ability to sketch buildings, bridges, cars—just about anything—from memory, with perfect perspective and exact detail, in just a few minutes. Oliver Sacks, who has observed the boy, speculates that Wilcher's autism somehow allows him to hold thousands of complex patterns in his mind simultaneously.

Another savant, Leslie Lemke, has the triple handicap of blindness, mental retardation, and cerebral palsy. Yet he has enthralled audiences around the world with his remarkable piano-playing abilities. He can play a piece of music flawlessly after hearing it only once, whether it is a sonata by Ludwig van Beethoven or a rock song by the Beatles. After listening to a forty-five-minute opera tape a single time, he can transpose the music to the piano and, as he plays, sing the opera's libretto—in the foreign language in which he heard it.

Both artistic and musical genius are common among savants. Many of them also display evidence of extra-sensory perception. In 1978, a San Diego psychologist by the name of Bernard Rimland published a study of the case histories of approximately 5,400 savant children from around the world. He determined that 561 of them, or a little more than 10 percent, exhibited signs of unusual perception. The parents of these special youngsters were usually the first to notice their child's inexplicable clairvoyance. "He seems to be very psychic," reported the parent of a boy savant who generally rode the school bus home. "We would decide to pick up George from school suddenly, if we were in the area. He would tell the teacher we were coming, and he would come to open the door when we arrived. So he has many special abilities, but cannot write his name or write a sentence." The parents of another savant reported how the youngster had "an extraordinary ability to hear conversations out of range of hearing, and to pick up thoughts not spoken."

Just how savants' brains differ from normal brains and enable them to do all they do is not clear. But psychiatrist Darold Treffert, a leading expert on savant syndrome, believes that the syndrome is caused by damage to the brain's left hemisphere, usually incurred before birth. To compensate for this damage, the right hemisphere becomes overdeveloped, growing larger than normal and assuming dominance of the entire brain. The imbalance can, in extreme cases, result in a savant—an individual whose right-brain skills are highly developed but whose left-brain abilities are only minimal.

Treffert stresses that the significance of savant syndrome "lies in our inability to explain it. The savants stand as a clear reminder of our ignorance about ourselves, especially about how our brains function. For no model of brain function, particularly memory, will be complete until it can include and account for this remarkable condition." Many other scientists concur with Treffert. It is through the study of such rare and enigmatic disorders, they believe, that the mysterious relationship between the three-pound mass of gray matter and the seemingly amorphous mind will someday become clear.

Art from Outsiders Looking In

The paintings hang in prestigious galleries around the world, and some artists acknowledge them as masterpieces. Brimming with vivid colors and distorted shapes, sometimes layered with allusive words or phrases, they might be products of an avant-garde movement devoted to raw emotionality. But the artists are not adherents of any school—in fact, their only common trait is mental illness.

Links between madness and creativity have fascinated medical specialists for centuries. Cesare Lombroso, an Italian criminologist and one of the first to advance a theory on the subject, suggested in the late 1800s that genius was a pathological state. He averred that only the absence of reason allowed access to hallucination and illusion, "a true source of artistic and literary inspiration." Later researchers discarded Lombroso's theory and saw the art of the mentally ill as a way to delve into the depths of the artists' unconscious minds. Forms and colors expressed each artist's emotional past, recurring themes changed with age or development of the illness, and a cure might extinguish the creativity altogether.

At one Austrian hospital, this so-called outsider art has spawned a unique experiment—a residence for more than a dozen mentally ill artists and poets. The Haus der Künstler (house of artists) in Gugging encourages and celebrates its residents' work. Widely shown and published, the art illuminates the artists' troubled minds and provides new perspectives on the world, viewed from outside the bounds of cultural—and cognitive—orthodoxy.

Two residents pose before the decorated south front of the Haus der Künstler (above), while three others stand at a second-floor window. The wall paintings are the highly personalized expressions of resident artists. Other styles predominate on the brightly painted east side of the building (right), where some of the artists have proudly signed their work.

Unique Creations from Troubled Talents

A small pavilion on a hillside, the Haus der Künstler is surrounded by meadows, fields, and woods. In this idyllic setting, mental patients paint, draw, and write in response to urges that may not be unlike those that drive artists everywhere.

The Haus der Künstler was founded in 1981 by Dr. Leo Navratil, the director of the psychiatric hospital in Gugging, who was impressed by the talent his patients displayed in diagnostic drawing tests. Navratil established an environment where their creativity would be given free rein; there are no studios, no fixed hours. The resulting work shows virtually no influence by other artists, reflecting only the personalities and dispositions of the individual residents.

Figures, emblems, and slogans crowd the walls and ceiling of August Walla's room in the Haus der Künstler (below). Dr. Navratil has said of Walla that he "lives in a permanent fear of death, God, spirits and man. Through his artwork, he has been able to fend off these dangers to a certain degree."

Humanized objects are common in the minutely detailed *Jungle* (top left) by Johann Garber. Garber uses a feather and india ink to completely fill every space on the page. Directly reflecting the artist's altered state of consciousness, the formalized figures in Oswald Tschirtner's untitled piece (above) have disproportionally large heads and long, legless bodies. The human form is also a major theme in Philipp Schöpke's *Family* (left). Schöpke's figures typically have oversize heads with rows of enormous teeth; they are often transparent, with ribs, heart and stomachs clearly visible.

As simple and flat as a prehistoric cave drawing, Stag by Franz Kernbeis (left) has a clearly human face. The abstract Self Portrait (below left on this page) by Fritz Koller incorporates recognizable fragments of human forms as well as geometric shapes—considered by some to demonstrate the disintegration of his personality. Tables (below), a work by Heinrich Reisenbauer, is an extreme example of formalization, a clear effort to impose order on a confused mind.

Common Threads in Uncommon Visions

The thoroughly individual styles of outsider artists share features that reflect the most dramatic (but not the most serious) symptoms of schizophrenia. Dr. Navratil identified three main characteristics—humanization, formalization, and symbolization—pervading his patients' art. In humanization, emotional attributes are displaced onto inanimate objects, which may have humanlike faces or be deformed in some telling way. Formalization, expressed in geometric forms or repetition of stereotyped patterns, reflects a yearning to restore structure to the disordered mind. Symbolization is the process by which humanized objects begin to assume a constant meaning in the artist's mind, at first mysterious but finally completely rational.

Two drawings on the theme of rockets (near right) reveal the months-long mood swings that characterize Johann Hauser's illness. In a manic state, the artist displays an expansive style, full of detail and bright colors and signed with great confidence; by contrast, the depressed Hauser produced a flat, static, monochromatic rocket. Woman with Feather Hat and Colorful Skirt (far right) illustrates the artist's approach to a favorite subject. Hauser's women are at once feminine and frightening, portrayed in bold, expressive colors with breasts that look like rockets.

A Manic-Depressive's Wild Swings of Style

The colorful drawings of Johann Hauser are among the most important works by outsider artists. A manic-depressive, Hauser was first committed to a hospital at age seventeen. He was thirty-three in 1959 when Dr. Navratil invited him to begin drawing, an activity he has pursued diligently ever since. His symptoms improved after he turned to art, but Hauser remains dependent on the hospital.

Hauser's art, which changes with the phases of his illness, manifests the deepest levels of his internal reality. He seems aware that his images are an effective way for him to reach out to others. In any event, Hauser's style is influential at Gugging, where his picture of a blue star on a white ground has become the symbol of the Haus der Künstler.

CHAPTER 3

A Crowd inside the Head

hen he was arrested near Columbus, Ohio, in 1977 for a series of rapes, twenty-two-year-old Billy Milligan seemed unsure of whether he was guilty. A high-school dropout who had recently lost his job as a maintenance worker, Milligan looked dazed and helpless. As he awaited trial, however, his demeanor changed often and dramatically. On two occasions he attempted suicide—once by banging his head against a wall, once by smashing a toilet bowl and cutting his wrists with the porcelain shards. Yet the same man watched with childish delight as cockroaches cavorted in his jail cell.

In a revealing series of interviews, psychologist Dorothy Turner uncovered the startling reason for Milligan's many moods. Billy himself, she found, was just one of several distinct personalities who alternately took control of the young man's body. In time, one alter ego confessed to committing the rapes, and others admitted having taken part in robberies. Still another—unaware of his companion selves and obviously bewildered—had been in control when the police took Billy Milligan into custody. As Turner and other experts later testified, each of Milligan's personalities could tell right from wrong—the classic legal criterion of sanity. But all of the selves put together did not add up to a whole person who could be held legally accountable. Billy Milligan, his lawyers and psychiatrists argued, was innocent of any wrongdoing, because no single personality was responsible for his body's actions.

In a verdict without precedent in American law, Judge Jay C. Flowers agreed. On December 4, 1978, William Milligan became the first American acquitted of major criminal charges on the grounds of multiple personality. And like many defendants deemed mentally incompetent, he was then committed to the state mental-health system for an indefinite term of treatment.

Along with Milligan, according to the psychologist and four psychiatrists who gave evidence in his defense, went a stunning variety of other selves. Arthur, a scholarly Briton who had been one of the first personalities to discover he was not alone, was the stage manager of the show, deciding which self should emerge at any given time. An avid reader, he was also one of the few Milligan personalities to require glasses. Ragen, a Yugoslav munitions specialist who could speak and write the Yugoslav language of Serbo-Croatian as well as English, protected the other personalities by taking control in threatening situations. A karate expert filled with hate, Ragen openly admitted to violent, even criminal behavior; his name was thought by psychiatrists to mean "rage again."

Still another ego, Tommy, was a combative teenager with a gift for Houdini-like escapes. He once wriggled out of a straitjacket in ten seconds. Three other teenage boys held a spot on the long list of selves, as did a tormented eight-year-old named David and two females: a dyslexic three-year-old and an introverted, nineteen-year-old lesbian who eventually confessed to the rapes. Nor was that the end of Milligan's astonishing cast of internal characters. Following the trial, his doctors discovered at least thirteen more.

Psychologist William James called the sense of self "the most puzzling puzzle with which psychology has to deal." Unusual mental states like that of Billy Milligan confound common-sense notions of personal identity. They also can lead to phenomena of behavior and experience stranger than anything concocted by fiction writers or reported in the annals of the paranormal.

Such exceptional cases suggest that the healthy, integrated mind is only the most familiar of several possible models. Still other remarkable minds differ from the norm by their superior abilities. Honored as creative geniuses and visionaries, such individuals

are often described as high strung and were once considered likely to crumble under the weight of their talents. Although that old association between madness and genius is now largely discredited, the minds of the gifted remain for the most part as much a mystery as those of individuals traditionally categorized as insane.

In different cultures or ages, the symptoms now ascribed to multiple personality or other mental illnesses were variously regarded as evidence of divine inspiration, demonic possession, or mediumistic trance. Hallucinations were believed to be otherworldly visions, while obsessive-compulsive behaviors were attributed to diabolic influence.

Today, most scientists who study aberrant mental functions place the blame squarely on physiological or psychological factors. Yet some echo the theories of an earlier time, suggesting that rare minds, such as those of multiple personalities, schizophrenics, and even creative geniuses, may be tapping into a universal mind, a higher reality where all objects and events are linked to all others. "It is at least possible," suggested Graham Reed, chairman of the psychology department at Toronto's York University, "that the schizophrenic symptom, as well as nirvana, unity, and so on, merely refer to the extremes of a continuum"—that all human beings may dwell along a line stretching between the egocentric individual and the selfless universal. In fact, some maverick psychiatrists have embraced the view that mental illness is not a door closed to reality as we know it but a door opening on an-

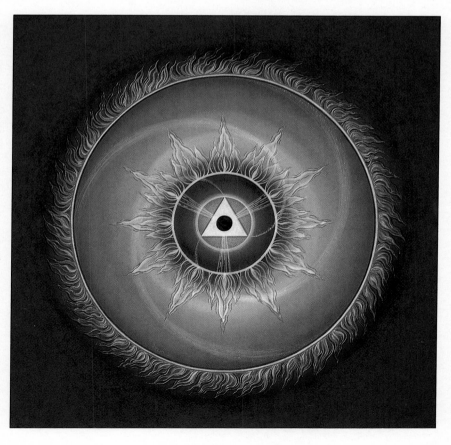

A puppeteer and his assistant pull the strings of their puppets in this drawing by a young art student who suffered a schizophrenic breakdown in the 1930s. Although the artist's intentions are unknown, the scene vividly illuminates the loss of control experienced by many schizophrenics.

Observed by an oversize cat, fiendish owls and bats assail the drowsy artist in Francisco de Goya's The Sleep of Reason Brings Forth Monsters. Intended primarily as an attack on the corrupt Spanish monarchy, the 1799 etching also suggests that an irrational mind is helpless against self-induced terrors.

other, hidden realm. A psychosis such as schizophrenia, they believe, can be viewed as a vision quest from which much can be learned, by the therapist as well as by the sufferer.

Perhaps the most alien and alienated of human minds are those diagnosed as schizophrenic. Trapped in a world lacking meaning and in bodies seemingly beyond their control, schizophrenics account for nearly 40 percent of the admissions to state and county mental hospitals in the United States. Describing the disconnected existence of these tortured souls, medical author Patrick Young wrote that such patients "are in, but not of, the society in which they live. Their minds are divorced from reality." Their days are a cascade of tormenting delusions, hallucinations, voices, and fears.

The literal meaning of the word *schizophrenia,* which is Greek for "splitting of the mind," gives rise to a traditional, but misleading, definition of the disease as "split personality." In reality, the personality of a schizophrenic is not so much split as absent. Especially in the early stages, a patient appears flat and emotionless, devoid of feeling. Psychiatrist Edwin Fuller Torrey of Saint Elizabeth's Hospital in Washington, D.C., described two of his emotionally blank schizophrenic patients as "polite, at times stubborn, but never happy or sad." Likening their actions to those of robots, he revealed how one patient had "set fire to his house and then sat down placidly to watch TV. When it was called to his atten-

tion that the house was on fire, he got up calmly and went outside."

The accounts that schizophrenics offer of their mental ordeals further illustrate this lack of personal identity. Asked one day how he was feeling, a patient replied, "It doesn't feel. He is existing among everything. Their head is sort of swimming." Such blurred self-images make it impossible for most schizophrenics to draw a human figure on paper or to imagine or daydream. Many report feeling like puppets under someone else's control. Schizophrenics also suffer from gaps in mental logic, sometimes described as a loosening of the links between thoughts. Cause and effect, subject and object, and other logical connections fail to mesh in the schizophrenic's splintered mind. What may appear instead is something psychiatrists call word salad. An example of one patient's tumbled thought processes, as recorded in his diary, appeared in a classic 1964 study of mental illness: "When you wish upon a star Red—stop amber—caution purple—be on look out Green—go ahead with what you are doing God help us to take advice from other people and show them we can take being talked about and not get mad or lose you temper."

Perhaps the most painful syndrome of the disease is paranoid schizophrenia. The mind of a paranoid schizophrenic is a tangle of terrors. He or she hallucinates, hears threatening voices, and fears mysterious, unseen enemies. A paranoid's phantom demons usually speak aloud rather than appearing as visions, and they rarely if ever go away.

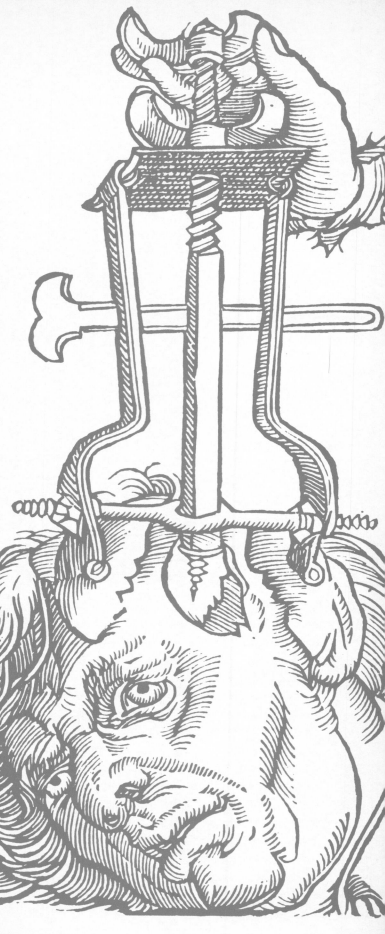

"Almost every day and every hour I hear voices about me," a 1907 case study quotes one patient as saying, "sometimes sounding from the wind, sometimes from footsteps, sometimes rattling dishes, from the rustling trees or from the wheels of passing trains."

Despite decades of research, the causes of schizophrenia remain a mystery. In the 1940s and early 1950s, European psychiatrists argued that the condition had an organic, or physical, cause within the brain. During the same period in the United States, a popular theory laid the blame instead on inadequate parents—so-called schizophrenogenic mothers who were either overprotective or rejecting, and fathers who were either too passive or too harsh.

Such psychosocial theories about schizophrenia were dealt a serious and perhaps fatal blow in the mid-1950s, however, when research at Saint Anne's Mental Hospital in Paris revealed that chlorpromazine, a drug that lowers the level of a brain chemical called dopamine, could reduce schizophrenic symptoms. To many, this suggested that the disease had a physical origin after all. More recently, investigators have discovered that the limbic system, the part of the brain responsible for emotions, is typically smaller in schizophrenics and that the cells of a schizophrenic's hippocampus—a part of the limbic system—are often seriously disorganized. Other studies have found that in many schizophrenic patients, the cavities filled with cerebrospinal fluid surrounding the brain are unusually large, indicating a smaller brain mass.

Further support for a physical cause comes from studies showing that one of ten children with a schizophrenic parent develops the disease; if both parents are afflicted, nearly half the children will become schizophrenic. Yet many researchers believe that heredity is only part of the explanation. "It might be a virus, an autoimmune disease, an inherited defect, prenatal damage, a neurotoxin, or a multitude of things," ventures psychiatrist Daniel Weinberger of the National Institute of Mental Health, near Washington, D.C. "I don't think there's just one cause."

Despite the modern focus on the medical causes of schizophrenia, some researchers still believe that social stresses may precipitate its onset. From his completion of psychoanalytic training in 1957 until his death in 1989, the well-known Scottish psychiatrist Ronald David Laing contended that schizophrenic patients are simply trying to escape from intolerable social or family pressures. In a famous aphorism, he described schizophrenia as a sane reaction to an insane world. An individual becomes schizophrenic, Laing wrote, when he "has come to feel he is in an untenable situation. He cannot make a move, or make no move, without being beset by contradictory and paradoxical pressures and demands, pushes and pulls. . . . He is, as it were, in a position of checkmate."

Laing and other writers have speculated that schizophrenia itself—in particular, the separation from the self or ego—may enable sufferers to enter a deeper emotional reality, an inner realm of experience from which others are barred. Describing untreated schizophrenia as a hazardous but potentially educational journey into "the infinite reaches of inner space," Laing contended that common treatments meant to disrupt the normal course of the disease, such as medication and electroshock therapy, may actually prevent the voyager from returning to the outer world.

As an alternative to the medical establishment's often ineffective remedies, Laing in 1965 established the first of several healing centers for the disease. In early 1991, one center in Littleton, New Hampshire, and a number of others in the United Kingdom remained active. There, doctors and schizophrenics lived together as equals, following the same rules. "You could call them sanctuaries, like bird sanctuar-

By drilling holes in the skull (left), a procedure known as trepanning, medieval physicians hoped to relieve pressure on the brain and cure certain forms of madness. Surprisingly, the patients often survived. By the seventeenth century, alchemical methods were used as therapy for mental illness; in the artist's spoof above, symbols of madness go up in smoke when a patient thrusts his head into an alchemist's furnace. In the nineteenth century, electricity was touted as a panacea. With the apparatus at right, nerve specialist Jean-Martin Charcot subjected 300 patients a day to mild electrical voltages—presaging the severe shock treatments of our own era.

A poet and practicing psycho-
therapist with an interest in
yoga, former military psychiatrist Ronald David Laing (left)
argued that schizophrenics
could be helped more by a
''caring'' atmosphere and respect than by psychoactive
drugs or other invasive thera-
pies. Laing's techniques remain
in use at several treatment
centers, including Burch House
(above) in New Hampshire.

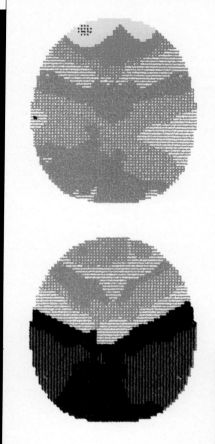

Differing by 99.7 percent according to a standard comparison, the so-called brain maps at left—which use shape and color to display brain-wave pattern and amplitude—reflect two selves of a woman with multiple personality disorder. In the top map, light blue tones reveal that a matronly personality, known as Rachael, generates relatively strong delta waves. Black and purple shades in the lower map indicate that the delta waves are faint or absent in the scan of her angry and suicidal basic self, "S."

Scribbled, printed, or carefully inscribed, the markedly different writing samples below represent only a few of the ninety-two personalities sharing the body of Truddi Chase. Before Chase became aware of her condition, still another personality retyped such manuscripts in order to conceal the variations in her handwriting.

radically as the alternate personalities took control.

In a follow-up study, Putnam found that blood-flow patterns in the brain also fluctuated as individuals moved from one identity to another, and a colleague of Putnam's discovered measurable differences in the voiceprints of separate personalities. The conclusion was remarkable: Just as the behaviors of various selves were unique to each individual, so too were their brain functions. Multiple personality disorder had been put on a firm scientific footing—almost a century after psychiatrists had first observed it.

That result would not have come as a surprise to the authors of an extraordinary book titled *When Rabbit Howls*, published in 1987. Written by the ninety-two selves who inhabit a woman known as Truddi Chase, the book presents a set of personalities who have chosen to remain divided. According to the personalities, who call themselves the Troops, the original Truddi Chase "went to sleep" when she was raped at the age of two and has never reawakened. Although that self did not die, they say, she also never grew up, remaining as innocent and inexperienced as any two-year-old child. As suggested by their joint authorship of the book, the selves inside Truddi Chase function effectively as a team, working a responsible but unidentified job as they make a type of communal life for themselves. Some remain articulate and adult, others wounded and childlike. The personality closest to the lost two-year-old self is known as Rabbit. Incapable of speech or writing, Rabbit—for whom the book is named—expresses the child's stored pain with an animal's anguished howls.

The public had a glimpse of the practical implications of such a complicated existence in November 1990, when a woman known only as Sarah unveiled six of her forty-six personalities during her testimony in a Wisconsin criminal case. Age twenty-seven at the time of the trial, Sarah, a trim Korean-American raised in Iowa, accused twenty-nine-year-old Mark Peterson of taking advantage of one of her less responsible selves—alleging, in legal terms, that he had knowingly had sex with a person "mentally unable to assess her conduct." For his part, Peterson admitted the sexual encounter but denied knowing at the time that Sarah was mentally ill.

On the witness stand, Sarah and her various selves provided compelling testimony. "Who would be in the best position to talk about that night?" prosecutor Joseph Paulus asked Sarah in a widely reported exchange.

"Franny," she replied.

"Would it be possible for us to meet Franny, and talk to her?"

"Yes," Sarah said. "Now?"

Without further ado, she dropped her chin, sat motionless for about five seconds, then looked straight at the prosecutor and murmured "Hel-lo." Franny had arrived.

Quickly sworn in by Judge Robert Hawley, Franny testified that she had met Peterson and that during their conversation had told him about her various identities. Later, she said, he asked to meet "the one who likes to have fun"—the self named Jennifer. "I went away," Franny recounted, and the childishly innocent Jennifer appeared. Following the thread of the story, the prosecutor then asked whether Jennifer could testify. In response, the witness closed her eyes and dipped her head again, then blinked and asked for a drink of water in a high-pitched voice.

After taking a sworn oath, Jennifer airily described her date with Peterson. She removed her shorts, she explained, "because he told me to." Asked if she objected to sex, she replied, "Tell me what sex is and I'll tell you if I objected." As the extraordinary testimony unfolded, the prosecutor summoned and questioned three more personalities—a six-year-old named Emily, a woman named Leslie, and an animal-like character named Sam who growled when he was afraid. Although Leslie and Sam had little to contribute, Emily testified that she had seen the sexual encounter, candidly confessing, "I was peeking the whole time." The day in court ended abruptly when Jennifer reappeared to announce she was hungry and wanted to go home.

On the basis of the personalities' testimonies, Peterson was convicted of the assault charge, but the verdict was

Painted after three years of psychoanalysis, this 1957 self-portrait by the multiple-personality sufferer known as Sybil employs blue watercolors to merge three women into one. Blue was Sybil's favorite color; she once said it represented all the shades of love.

later overturned because defense attorneys had been unable to conduct a pretrial psychiatric examination of Sarah. The state subsequently decided against a retrial to avoid subjecting the fragile young woman to further distress.

Uncanny enough in its own right, multiple personality disorder has also been repeatedly linked to paranormal phenomena. Certain researchers, for instance, believe that not all the selves manifested by a multiple are internally generated. Some, they venture, may be spirits from another realm, or as one therapist suggested, the vestiges of past lives. In the 1980s, American psychiatrist Ralph Allison coined the term Inner Self Helper to describe a special entity that helps the patient to heal and reintegrate. Personalities of this type often claim to be conduits for divine love and healing power, and Allison suggests they may in fact enter the patient from an out-

side beneficent power. "There is always a logical reason for the alter personality's existence," Allison believes. "Thus the discovery of an entity who doesn't serve any recognizable purpose presents a diagnostic problem. Such entities often refer to themselves as spirits. Over the years I've encountered too many such cases to dismiss the possibility of spirit possession completely."

Truddi Chase, for example, counts among her ninety-two personalities one named Ean, who has a rich brogue and a vivid memory of a past life in Ireland. Wise and well balanced, he looks after the other selves. "Who is Ean, really?" wrote Chase's psychologist, Robert Phillips, in an afterword to *When Rabbit Howls*. "He seems to be part of the Troops—yet also is separate from them. It is said that Ean sits 'above.' He works powerfully behind the scenes, and he emanates great energy. It is also said of him that he is not only of this time but also timeless."

An equally mysterious Inner Self Helper became a key factor in the recovery of multiple personality sufferer Kit—short for Katherine—Castle. As chronicled by author Stefan Bechtel in the 1989 book *Katherine, It's Time*, Castle began undergoing treatment for MPD in New York State in the 1980s. As with many other multiples, therapy revealed that her core self had begun to shatter during childhood. Among her resident personalities, Castle apparently hosted a guardian angel named Michael, who was described by various selves who had seen and heard him as a kindly man in a dark hat and coat. Michael first appeared on the day that a family friend who had provided emotional support for the young Kit died before her eyes, killed in a stock-car racing crash.

Many years later, explains Bechtel, a personality called Me-Liz saw

William "Billy" Milligan smiles shyly in a snapshot (below) taken in 1981 at a maximum-security psychiatric hospital. By then his gentle demeanor hid twenty-three distinct personalities—some mature, some criminal, and some childishly sweet. Allen, one of several artists among them, drew and painted these portraits of six of the other personalities. Fourth from the left is Adalana, a young woman who was the only personality implicated in the rapes that occasioned Milligan's commitment to the Ohio state mental-health system in 1978.

Arthur, Milligan's most responsible personality, spoke with a British accent, read and wrote Arabic, and enjoyed medical books. Distant, unemotional, and extremely intelligent, he arbitrated disputes among the other personalities.

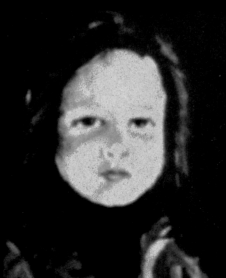

Four years old, deaf, and possibly retarded, Shawn was one of thirteen suppressed selves that Arthur considered "undesirable." On rare occasions, Shawn emerged anyway, making a buzzing sound so that he could feel the vibration in his head.

Three-year-old Christine, shown clutching her favorite rag doll, was an intelligent little girl with dyslexia who liked to draw butterflies and flowers. In a note to Milligan's attorney Judy Stevenson, this personality once asked why she had to stay "in a cage" when she wanted to go out and play.

Michael on a Virginia seashore, "absurdly overdressed in the heat, wearing a dark coat, dark trousers, and holding a dark hat in his hands." He was not alone. "Behind and above him, hanging in the air like three flashing, ghostly cymbals, were the beings." According to Me-Liz, Michael had told Castle to expect these ghostly visitations, "that they would signify a great new unfolding in her life. Something grand and wonderful was preparing to take place."

As therapy progressed, Michael and the beings of light who accompanied him acted as partners in the process of healing, convincing Castle's selves to fuse into one. The process came to its logical climax in what Castle now refers to as the "final farandola," an intense, all but indescribable experience of bright lights and a whirling sensation supervised by Michael; Castle emerged from the event alone.

Views on Michael's identity, and that of other Inner Self Helpers, vary. Psychiatrist Cornelia Wilbur, who helped treat Castle, suggests that Michael was simply a projection or mental image. "Being able to visualize the Inner Self Helper is a way of preserving its integrity, its separateness," Wilbur has commented. "It's a way of saying, 'This has nothing to do with me, it is someone completely outside of me, helping me.' " On the other hand, Kit Castle's minister, Kaye DeYoung, is equally convinced that Michael was indeed a separate being. "I considered Michael to be an angel. I believe in angels," he wrote. "I know God speaks, and he speaks to people in different ways." For his part, Joseph Pearce, author of *The Crack in the Cosmic Egg*, has compared the Inner Self Helper to the Buddhist concept of the *tulpa*, a phantasmic spirit-self that passes on from one generation to the next. Usually hidden from the conscious persona, the protective being sometimes emerges during the rigorous training undergone by Tibetan monks.

Whatever the origin of their various selves, people with multiple personality disorder seem exceptionally open to paranormal events of many kinds. Chris Sizemore, the original "Eve," for example, repeatedly experienced what she described as precognitive visions. She alleged that on one occasion she convinced her husband to stay home because of a fear he would be electrocuted; a co-worker who

Beautiful as a Renaissance Madonna, nineteen-year-old Adalana was a lesbian who yearned for love and intimacy—urges that allegedly caused her to commit three rapes using Milligan's body. Unlike any of the other personalities, she suffered from nystagmus, a medical condition in which the eyes involuntarily dart back and forth.

The first self to reveal Milligan's multiple personality disorder, eight-year-old David endured pain and suffering for all of the alter egos. Perhaps as a result, he was often confused and had a short attention span. This is a detail from David's portrait; Allen painted him small, in one corner of an otherwise featureless canvas, suggesting the isolation of an abused child.

Nineteen years old, with a Boston accent, April was regarded by the other selves as insane because of her violent plans for revenge against the man she believed abused Billy Milligan as a child. Despite her differences with the others, she helped with sewing and other housework.

According to Kit Castle, a woman who recovered from multiple personality disorder in 1986, hazy lights always appeared in photographs of her "Me-Liz" personality—including the one above, taken at a party. An alleged psychic, Me-Liz was one of several Castle personalities who reported encounters with a guardian angel named Michael, depicted in a sketch by Castle at right. A compassionate figure who comforted Castle as a child, Michael claimed to come from her "real father" in the sky. "When you turn on the porch light in your heart," the little girl heard him say, "He'll send me to help you."

took his place that day was indeed electrocuted on the job. Similarly, Billy Milligan's family reportedly was accustomed to the fact that Billy seemed to sense when his sister was in trouble, even when she was hundreds of miles away.

By some accounts, multiple personalities also seem to generate or absorb vast amounts of energy, physical and psychic. Psychiatrist Ralph Allison has remarked on being psychically sapped of vitality by a woman patient with multiple personalities. Truddi Chase's therapist, Robert Phillips, experienced just the opposite effect, feeling abnormally well and energetic after each meeting with her. Yet in *When Rabbit Howls,* Chase's personalities report a persistent problem with light bulbs and car batteries—left in their vicinity, say the selves, both items very soon go dead. On an even more dramatic note, a nineteenth-century source tells of an apparent multiple named Mollie Fancher—also known as the Brooklyn Enigma—who was said to kill small pets by draining their life force.

Psychic researcher Scott Rogo reported that he asked Ralph Allison how many of those afflicted with MPD seem to have paranormal abilities. "Every one of them," the psychiatrist responded. "It may be the primary personality that has some ability to tell what's coming up in the future for her kids, or accidents they're going to get into. That happens quite frequently. . . . If the patient has a lot of personalities, there will be one who is very psychic, and the others will have average ability or no abilities."

In addition to their supposed psychic powers, people with MPD tend to be unusually creative, typically harboring musicians, painters, and authors among their many egos. But the condition itself is perhaps the ultimate creative answer to unbearable reality. In the face of childhood anguish, those with multiple personalities did not retreat into psychosis. Instead, each invented new selves to share the horror in a painful but necessary triumph over tragedy.

The idea of a link between creativity and mental instability is certainly nothing new. "The lunatic, the lover and the poet," Shakespeare wrote in *A Midsummer Night's Dream,* "are of imagination all compact." A generation later, the poet John Dryden agreed. "Great wits are sure to madness near allied," he wrote, "and thin partitions do their bounds divide." For his part, the French author Marcel Proust stated flatly that "everything great comes from neurotics," among whom he evidently included himself. "They alone," he said, "have founded religions and composed our masterpieces."

By the nineteenth century, the link between genius and insanity was accepted scientific dogma. French psychiatrist Moreau de Tours contended that both states stemmed from mental overactivity. Cesare Lombroso, an Italian physician and early criminologist, saw genius as a psychosis related to epilepsy. And in the 1890s a British doctor named John Nisbet concluded that genius and madness were simply different phases of a "morbid susceptibility" that resulted from an imbalance in the cerebrospinal system.

William James, however, strongly disagreed. There was no accepted definition of genius, he declared, and no evidence that insanity was more common among the brilliant and accomplished. In the end, statistical surveys bore him out; mental illness occurs as commonly in the population as a whole as it does among the gifted few. Yet the roll call of great minds clouded by mental illness is a long one, an extraordinary compendium of struggles waged simultaneously against inner demons and real-world adversity. The great seventeenth-century mathematician and physicist Isaac Newton, for instance, fell victim at the age of fifty to a paranoid breakdown that incapacitated him for a year and a half. Chronically absent-minded and quarrelsome, Newton had trouble eating and sleeping for several months prior to the episode. He accused friends of conspiring against him and claimed to hear conversations no one else could. One reputable biographer has since speculated that Newton, a lifelong bachelor who showed little interest in women, lost his mental bearings because of suppressed homosexual impulses. Psychiatrist and author Anthony Storr suggests instead that Newton's midlife paranoia stemmed from the effects of his having been abandoned by his mother when he was a three-year-old child.

Another Englishman, the brilliant eighteenth-century writer and scholar Samuel Johnson, was prey to such black depressions that he once instructed his housekeeper to lock him in his room and place him in chains if he became demented. Johnson also practiced various obsessive-compulsive rituals. On passing through a doorway, reported a woman friend, he "would give a sudden spring and make such an extensive stride as if trying for a wager how far he could stride." He also stepped over cracks in paving stones and touched every pole when walking along a road.

More than a century later, Winston Churchill, the prime minister of England during World War II, found himself at the mercy of what he called his "black dog"—abject depressions. As a child, Churchill was shunted from one boarding school to another by a socialite mother and politician father who had scant time for him. His letters home were pathetic pleas for visits and mail he rarely received. Psychiatrist Storr believes that Churchill grew up convinced that only by doing exceptional things could he earn the love and respect he craved; his ferocious energy, according to Storr, was fueled by the fear that despair would overtake him if he stopped to rest. In slack periods, Churchill sank into a melancholy that he escaped only intermittently through writing and painting; late in his life, the once-dynamic wartime leader and eloquent orator sat alone for hours at a time in what amounted to a depressive stupor. "I have achieved a great deal," he said to his daughter Diana, "to achieve nothing in the end."

Although individual examples such as Newton, Johnson, and Churchill cannot outweigh the statistics showing no consistent link between madness and genius, a few scientists wonder if the two mental conditions may stem from a similar source. Research has shown, writes psychiatrist Storr, that "some psychological characteristics which are inherited as part of the predisposition to schizophrenia are divergent, loosely associative styles of thinking which, when normal, are 'creative.'" Similarly,

Author Mary Shelley (above), the creator of Victor Frankenstein and his monster (right), wrote that the enduring story "sprang from a waking dream of extraordinary vividness"—said by many to be a common source of creativity. Shelley's vision blended horror with a recent discovery: that electricity could make dead frog legs twitch as though restoring them to life.

psychiatrist Roland Fischer of Washington, D.C.'s Georgetown University believes that the hallucinations that are symptoms of madness in some people are mystical founts of creativity in others. He calls such experiences "communications with the unknown."

The father of psychoanalysis himself, Sigmund Freud, struggled to explain the roots of creativity. "Analysis," he once confessed, "can do nothing toward elucidating the nature of the artistic gift, nor can it explain the means by which the artist works." He concluded that artists are simply better than most people at channeling fantasies into something useful. But since, in Freud's view, fantasy is an unhealthy escape from reality—"a happy person never fantasizes"—artists are by his definition unhappy and unhealthy.

Asked to supply their own explanation of the creative process, poets, musicians, and other artists often ascribe inspiration to a power outside themselves. Just as the Greeks spoke of the muses—the nine goddesses of the arts—John Milton wrote of a "celestial patroness" who dictated to him what he modestly called "my unprecedented verse." British Romantic poet Percy Bysshe Shelley seems to have shared a similar experience. "A man cannot say, 'I will compose poetry,' " he wrote, "for the mind in creation is as a fading coal, which some invisible influence, like an inconstant wind, awakens to transitory brightness."

William Thackeray, the author of *Vanity Fair* and other popular nineteenth-century works, remarked that it sometimes seemed "as if an occult power was moving the pen." The character, he said, "does or says something and I ask, how the dickens did he come to think of that?" Similarly, the novelist Mary Ann Evans, who wrote under the pseudonym George Eliot, said that in her best writing she felt that her personality became a mere instrument for a "spirit" that took possession of her.

Such descriptions of creative automatism abound in the world of music as well. The precocious eighteenth-century genius Wolfgang Amadeus Mozart declared in an oft-quoted letter that he heard compositions in his head before he wrote them down. They arrived almost fully formed, he said. "Nor do I hear in my imagination the parts successively, but I hear them, as it were, all at once." To occupy his conscious mind while he transmitted the sounds to paper, Mozart sometimes asked his wife, Constanze, to read to him as he composed. Four generations later, the Russian composer Peter Ilyich Tchaikovsky paid his own tribute to a subconscious inner force. When in the throes of creation, he said, "I forget everything and behave like a madman. Everything within me starts pulsing and quivering."

The same ungovernable force also seems to affect

The manuscript below, a minuet composed and transcribed by Wolfgang Amadeus Mozart at the tender age of four, is evidence of his remarkable genius. Here pictured seated at the keyboard at six years old, Mozart said he received his compositions "complete and finished" in his mind.

MYS: MIND AND BEYOND

Matthias Grünewald's The
Temptation of Saint Anthony
depicts horrific visions sent by
Satan to distract the devout
hermit. Like Saint Anthony,
those known as fantasy-prone
personalities find their minds
obsessed with detailed fancy
instead of real-world fact. Unlike him, most seem to enjoy it.

those who perform music. To describe her most intense state of artistic immersion and creativity, concert violinist Nadja Salerno-Sonnenberg refers to "the zone," a phrase athletes often use to identify the consciousness level that leads to peak performance. The zone, she says, is "a heightened feeling where everything is right. Everything comes together. Everything is one. Everybody agrees. Everybody is with you and you, yourself, are not battling yourself. It's very, very rare."

Such accounts may refer, some experts believe, to a level of awareness suspended between the conscious and the unconscious. Carl Jung identified a similar mental state as the "primordial" mind; others call it reverie. In the 1960s, Harold Rugg, a researcher at Columbia University, dubbed this misty middle ground the "transliminal mind," a condition he associated not only with creativity but also with the meditative states of Eastern religions, light hypnotic trances, intuition, and hypnagogic states—those periods between sleep and wakefulness. Whatever this state is called, its chief attribute is an uncritical ambiance of relaxed readiness and receptivity. Open to any and all ideas, the transliminal mind eventually finds the simplest image or set of symbols that solve the creative problem confronting it, said Rugg. The result is a seemingly magical creative flash.

Creative artists have always had ways of courting the inspirational state. In a recipe similar to that followed by many another author, Samuel Johnson required a purring cat, an orange peel, and a cup of tea to write. Rudyard Kipling needed dark black ink; Proust labored in a soundproof room; and the Baltimorean sage H. L. Mencken washed his hands dozens of times daily. The German dramatist and poet J. C. Friedrich von Schiller was able to detect the muse in the odor of rotting apples, and he always kept some handy.

Linked by most neurologists to the right hemisphere of the brain—the province of imagination, intuition, and visual rather than verbal concepts—creativity has also been associated in some studies with theta waves, one of four general categories of brain waves. Researchers at the Menninger

Foundation in Kansas have found a resemblance between the mental images described by creative people and the vivid, sometimes mystical visions experienced by volunteers trained to produce theta waves. Other scientists have noted that theta waves are often associated with rage and violence—a modern reappearance of the old notions connecting genius and madness.

In recent years, neurologists have also identified at least one disorder apparently linked to musical talent: Tourette's syndrome, a neurological condition that begins with facial and muscular tics and progresses to uncontrollable outbursts of obscenity, imitations, and outlandish remarks. Neurologist and author Oliver Sacks treated a Tourette's patient who was a talented drummer, famous for wild riffs ignited by a tic or a compulsive rat-a-tat. Sacks found a drug that quieted the man's symptoms, at the cost of his musical virtuosity. The patient compromised, taking the medicine during the week but not on weekends.

Yet another musician, pianist-songwriter Connie Cook of Peoria, Illinois, claimed to have acquired her abilities by still another means—albeit one at which many would scoff. Cook reports that one night in 1981 she dreamed of friendly aliens from the Pleiades star cluster; a month later, she began compulsively writing songs. Before that, she says, she could not play a note, but now "music just flows out of me." She became a professional pianist, playing in a Peoria singles bar. Whatever the explanation, Cook has clearly tapped into a talent she had previously lacked. Her sister Carolyn, who rejects the UFO story, concedes that when Connie plays, "those aren't her fingers on the keys."

Although scorned by her sister, Cook's dream of an alien encounter would likely get a warmer reception from the highly creative mental minority known as fantasy-prone personalities. These are natural visionaries who live out much of their lives in one or more alternate realities of their own invention. By some accounts, they may make up as much as four percent of the population.

Fantasy-prone personalities first attracted scientific notice in the 1960s, when a Stanford University researcher,

Josephine Hilgard, began a study of good hypnotic subjects and the traits they have in common. To her surprise, Hilgard discovered that the best subjects almost always enjoyed extraordinarily vivid fantasy lives. Intrigued by that finding, Boston psychologists Theodore Barber and Sheryl Wilson interviewed another twenty-seven highly receptive hypnotic subjects. All but one had profoundly detailed imaginary existences. Many spent as much as 95 percent of their waking moments in realms of their own creation.

Further research by Ohio University psychologist Steven Jay Lynn helped profile the typical fantasy-prone personality. Evenly divided between males and females, fantasy-prone individuals represent a cross section of age and personality type. One in four, says Lynn, shows signs of mental disturbance; one in ten has trouble turning off their fantasies long enough to perform daily tasks. Yet the condition also serves a critical stabilizing role. Lynn found that fantasies "contributed to psychological well-being" by helping the individuals cope with adversity and stress.

The elaborate inner lives of the fantasy prone are of a far different order than daydreams. Fully three-quarters of the group, for instance, are able to reach sexual climax by fantasy alone. "When I 'go away' I'm very definitely there and not here," one woman explained to an *Omni* magazine reporter. "I touch other people, other things, hear them, laugh, dance, talk, cry, scream, get scared, see and know everything that's going on."

Their constant imagining apparently makes fantasy-prone people hypersensitive to drugs, emotional stress, and even popular entertainment. Movies may be indistinguishable from reality. "To me it's real," the same woman remarked. "I scream or hyperventilate. . . . When I saw *Rambo* I ended up hiding under my seat." The fantasy prone may also experience a wide range of psychic phenomena—or, perhaps, fantasies of such phenomena. In their study, Barber and Wilson found that fantasy-prone subjects often reported clairvoyant dreams, out-of-body experiences, past-life regressions, and other brushes with the paranormal.

In 1988, *Omni* magazine attempted to get an inside look at the condition by asking several fantasy-prone personalities for details of their current scenarios. Among the results was a 2,500-word epic by a woman from Oregon. Much as a movie fan might watch a videotape over and over again, searching out favorite scenes, she claimed to have run the fantasy footage over and over in her mind for several years. In short, the fantasy begins with the woman walking alone in a strange forest. She comes upon a group of people with golden skin and bright orange eyes and learns that they are slaves. A woman she befriends teaches her their language, and in the evenings she listens to eerie music played on odd-looking instruments.

Eventually, she and her friend escape to the rocky realm of the "northern people." Along the way she eats a fruit whose taste and texture she can describe to the last seed: "fleshy and very sweet," she reports, "a bit like a melon but with a slightly rancid taste." In time, they find the northerners, who have long gray hair and gray eyes and wear medieval clothes. After a stint as a potato peeler, the woman is granted an audience with the bejeweled king; his gems are "quite lovely," she adds, "but nothing extremely flashy." The king treats her kindly and offers to make her a scribe. But then she meets an alien who wants her to travel to his planet as a sort of ambassador trainee. She decides to go. And there it ends.

Although fantasy-prone personalities are usually able to harness their extraordinary imaginations, they cannot simply break the narrative habit. Like those with schizophrenia, multiple personality disorder, or even exceptional artistic talent, the fantasy prone cannot take the human mind for granted. For them, its possibilities and limitations are the stuff of ordinary life. But in the daily mental struggle, those gifted or burdened with rare minds may capture a reality that more comfortable mentalities will never see. As psychiatrist Ronald David Laing wrote in 1967, "The ego is the instrument for living in this world. If the ego is broken up or destroyed, then the person may be exposed to other worlds, 'real' in different ways."

Time Out of Mind

Individuality itself seemed to dissolve and fade away into boundless being," wrote Alfred, Lord Tennyson; "death was an almost laughable impossibility." The poet had experienced a mystical trance, a rapturous feeling that his soul had soared free of his body. It was, he affirmed, "not a confused state but the clearest, the surest of the sure, utterly beyond words." Tennyson was not alone in treasuring such an experience.

Every culture in every age has recognized and prized this exalted condition. The revered oracles of ancient Greece delivered their prophecies while in trances, and religious mystics through the ages have sought revelatory visions in the same way. The behavior of the entranced—whose gaze may seem riveted on a vision unperceived by others—demonstrate that entrancement is a kind of changed reality: in effect, an altered state of being.

The ancient adventure comes in many forms. Mind-altering drugs may induce trances, but their use can be dangerous as well as illegal. One medical researcher has evoked trance sensations in volunteers by placing special magnets over their heads. However, as the examples on these pages indicate, achieving trances does not require elaborate equipment or special substances. Most are produced through simple but well-practiced physical and mental methods, ranging from wild dancing to quiet, intense meditation.

Whatever its origin, entrancement always entails a suspension of part of the brain's normal functioning, a splitting of consciousness. Everyday awareness of time, change, and death is interrupted, often yielding place to a sublime sense of immortality.

In an ecstatic trance, the minister of a snake-handling sect allows a poisonous copperhead to coil about his head at a 1948 gathering in Durham, North Carolina. Believing themselves protected by their faith, the pastor and his flock reported that they were rarely bitten.

When Faith Transcends All

Ecstatic trances are for many people a vital part of religious experience, a way to seek union with the Divine. Devotees of many faiths pursue heightened mystical states through regimens of spiritual devotion and physical purification. The word *mystical* itself comes from a Greek word meaning "to initiate into mystery," into a secret cult.

Many rituals, fasts, and celebrations are meant to help believers attain entrancement. The snake-handling ceremony above, for instance, is performed only after two hours of insistent chanting and cymbal clashing, an entrancing rhythmic din that, some say, lulls the snakes as well as the worshipers into altered states.

Extraordinary occurrences are said to accompany such trances. In most religions, believers have reportedly levitated, gained healing powers, or spontaneously developed physical marks of their faith on their bodies. Spiritual mentors often warn novices not to be seduced by such marvels; they are mere distractions from the true goal of oneness with the Divine.

Saint Catherine of Siena is transfixed by religious ecstasy in this eighteenth-century portrait by Tiepolo. It was said that during a trance she felt the pain of Christ's cruci-fixion as bleeding wounds— called the stigmata—appeared on her own palms and head.

A Haitian voodoo worshiper dances in a trance, as evi-denced by her staring eyes. In voodoo belief, everyday reality masks a spirit world; through ritual drumming, chanting, and dancing, worshipers hope to reach that world and become possessed by gods and spirits.

Surpassing the Body's Limitations

The mind power tapped in trances can lead to remarkable physical accomplishments, feats that seem to rewrite the body's ordinary rules. Many religious regimens use mastery of physical challenges as a step toward the Divine. Some say entrancement is the reason Hindus and others are able to walk barefoot across red-hot coals.

Even with no religious context, the mind power released in a trance can build remarkable physical skills. One American entertainer, strongman Joseph L. Greenstein, "The Mighty Atom," used a kind of trance power to bend iron bars and drive nails with his bare hands. Before performing, he would command the iron: "I am man, you are metal. My will is superior to you. You will bend, you will break."

Western medicine has also discovered the mind-body connection. Amid mounting evidence that states of mind can affect the body's functioning, several cancer clinics teach relaxation and visualization—trance-inducing techniques to help patients strengthen their bodies' defenses against disease.

Tibetan monks wrapped in wet, ice-cold sheets practice Tumo yoga in 40-degree temperatures. During motionless meditation, captured on film in 1985 by Harvard's Herbert Benson, each man purposefully raised his body temperature enough to dry his sheet in forty minutes. They perform the same ritual outdoors in the snow and on cold nights. While Westerners are dazzled by this practice, the monks value it simply as a means of fiery internal purification, leading to a higher state of consciousness.

Culminating an annual Hindu festival in Ceylon, barefoot devotees walk across an eighteen-foot bed of burning embers. Drumming that accompanies the ceremony is said to help the participants enter a state of religious trance.

A Hindu sadhu, or holy man, practices a rare form of meditation, with his head buried in sand, during a 1989 festival at the holy city of Allahabad, India. Deliberately slowing his breathing and heartbeat enabled him to hold this pose for hours. Sadhus perfect such feats as a spiritual discipline.

Grigory Rasputin, here seated among rapt admirers, cast an entrancing spell over the court of Russian czar Nicholas II, especially the women. A jealous prince wrote that Rasputin's eyes shone with "phosphorescent light," and the prince felt himself "falling into the power of this mysterious man."

Newspaper heiress Patricia Hearst strikes a militant pose before the emblem of the Symbionese Liberation Army, a radical group that kidnapped her in 1974. When she joined her captors in armed robbery and kidnapping, her parents insisted she had been brainwashed—in effect, entranced.

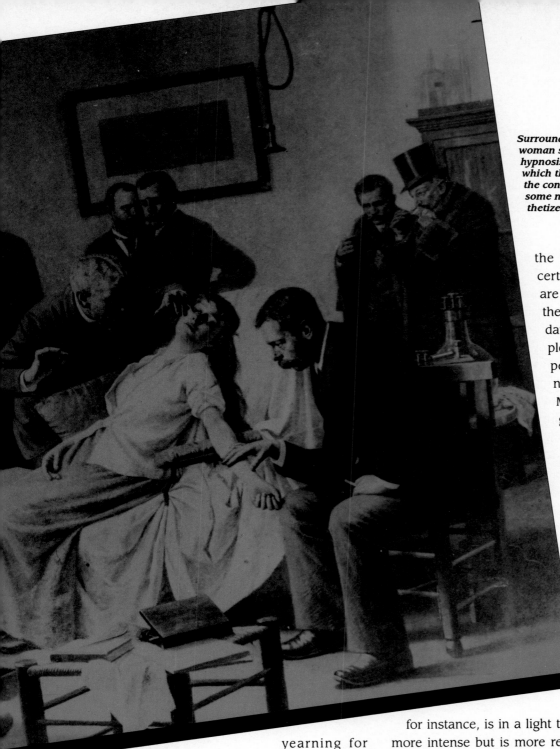

Surrounded by concerned physicians, a woman swoons into the sleeplike trance of hypnosis in this 1893 painting. A state in which the subconscious seems to dominate the conscious mind, hypnosis was used by some nineteenth-century doctors to anesthetize and to treat nervous disorders.

As William James pointed out, the various altered states share certain qualities; the differences are mainly of intensity. Whether they get there by way of whirling dances or meditation, many people in altered states of mind experience a sense of timelessness and physical lightness. Many report being suffused in a golden glow that stretches from horizon to horizon. Paradoxically, the altered state also often produces a narrowed focus of attention, a zeroing in on specifics.

In the continuum of consciousness, a trance, whether spontaneous or hypnotic, is an extension of daydreaming; meditation, though voluntary and purposeful, is hard to distinguish from a trance. A moviegoer who becomes oblivious to everything but the screen, for instance, is in a light trance; his or her awareness is more intense but is more restricted than in ordinary consciousness. Marijuana users have described their increased internal focus and detachment from the outside world with the analogy of an old-fashioned telephone switchboard in which all but one or two of the incoming trunk lines have been disconnnected.

When the power of such a state increases and the scope of consciousness narrows, unusual phenomena begin to appear, such as the blocking of pain signals. A deep trance—one induced by hypnosis, for example—can in some cases substitute for chemical anesthesia during major

yearning for transcendental enlightenment led many people to seek it through other means. Some focused on the demanding, ascetic way of Eastern mystics; others hoped to expand the mind's borders through science and technology. In recent decades a brand-new frontier of inquiry has been opened by the ever-growing ability of computers to mimic functions that had long been thought unique to the human mind. Still others embraced more mundane efforts at mind expansion, including sleep, daydreaming, trance, and hypnosis.

surgery. Apparently the patient's consciousness is so tightly focused that the pain generated by the surgeon's knife is momentarily outside the boundary of consciousness.

Most altered states also produce a major change in the sense of ego—a person's routine awareness of existing as a discrete entity. With the onset of a reverie, for instance, the monitoring self disappears; when the daydreamer snaps back to the here and now, the individual wonders where he or she has been for the past few minutes. Precisely this forgetfulness of self is at the core of some religions and systems of mind development.

Zen Buddhists sometimes use archery as a spiritual exercise. According to Zen master D. T. Suzuki, the meditating archer "ceases to be conscious of himself as the one who is engaged in hitting the bull's eye which confronts him." Ideally, the archer eliminates the distinctions between himself, the bow, the arrow, and the target, so that hitting the target is no more difficult than reaching out and touching it. In Zen, the goal is not physical success, but the state of mind required to achieve it. Nevertheless, the capacity to forget oneself is an important factor in perfecting any skill. A true master—artisan, artist, performer—forsakes the ego-centered focus of normal waking consciousness and becomes "lost in the work," much as John Bennett did during his exercises at Gurdjieff's institute.

Although various ancient cultures in the search for revelation have used what in today's jargon are called controlled substances—such as the soma of the Hindus—it is a fairly recent preoccupation in the West to view medications that affect the mind as tools for scientifically exploring higher consciousness. Many reputable researchers have worked to prove that mental changes produced by these psychoactive drugs can provide insight into the brain's perceptual equipment and illuminate normally shadowy parts of the psyche. They have a complicated task.

In the period following World War II, well before the serious physical and emotional side effects of drug use were so widely known, researchers began to tinker with a class of drugs called hallucinogenics. They discovered that these substances, including drugs such as psilocybin and lysergic acid diethylamide—which entered everyday language during the 1960s as LSD—were capable of producing powerful hallucinations in tiny doses. The first documented LSD "trip," as the mind-expanding excursions later became known, was made in 1943 by a Swiss chemist named Albert Hofmann, who took a mere quarter of a milligram of the drug and stumbled into a realm of startling revelation. "To see the flowers in my own garden is to see all the mystical wonder of creation," Hofmann marveled after his pioneering experiment.

Later researchers followed up on Hofmann's beatific experience, often with much broader goals in view. Much of the early funding for experiments in the United States, in fact, came from government agencies. The Central Intelligence Agency, interested in the hallucinogenics' potential as weapons that could break down the defenses of enemy agents and unlock the lips of trained spies, in the early 1950s subsidized studies in which witting and unwitting subjects—sometimes CIA officials themselves—were given food or drink laced with drugs such as LSD. Their research revealed that in addition to causing kaleidoscopic visions, the drugs at times seemed to produce effects similar to psychosis. Yet the testing continued in one form or another until the mid-1960s. By then, however, agency officials had to admit that while LSD penetrated the innermost reaches of the mind, it unleased such a gamut of human reactions and emotions that even the most skilled manipulator could not claim control over the minds of those who ingested it.

Aldous Huxley, a British novelist and philosopher, tested the effects of cactus-derived mescaline on his own psyche and recorded his observations in the 1954 essay *The Doors of Perception,* which took its title from William Blake. Huxley recounted floods of pleasurable sensations, such as "a slow dance of golden lights," and described the flashes of "transcendental otherness" he experienced while riding in a car through a Los Angeles suburb under the drug's in-

Bizarre apparitions assail a young man under the mind-altering influence of ether. Such alarming hallucinations were among the unpleasant side effects that led physicians to abandon ether as a general anesthetic soon after its discovery in the mid-1800s, around the time this etching was made.

fluence. A stucco wall with a slanting shadow across it, for example, was "blank but unforgettably beautiful, empty but charged with all the meaning and the mystery of existence. The revelation dawned and was gone again within a fraction of a second."

The incredible flow of sensory information let loose by the mescaline led Huxley to the hypothesis that the main function of the brain and nervous system is that of a reducing valve to restrict the input of reality to a manageable level. He surmised that so much data is available through the five senses that if all of it were processed the mind would be overwhelmed, incapable of dealing with the problems of everyday life.

The mescaline, Huxley believed, disabled the brain's filtering function, allowing the mind to become flooded with mental events that are usually excluded because they have no survival value. These intrusions, he wrote, are "biologically useless, but aesthetically and sometimes spiritually valuable." He believed them to be representations of what he called Mind at Large, an awareness of everything happening everywhere in the universe. Furthermore, he suggested, they can be stimulated by a catalyst other than drugs, such as illness, fatigue, fasting, or complete sensory withdrawal in a dark, silent place.

Whatever the means of achieving them, Huxley believed that humanity needed these "artificial paradises." He opined that "most men and women lead lives at the worst so painful, at the best so monotonous, poor and limited that the urge to escape, the longing to transcend themselves if only for a few moments, is and has always been one of the principal appetites of the soul. Art and religion, carnivals and saturnalia, dancing and listening to oratory—all these have served, in H. G. Wells's phrase, as Doors in the Wall. And for private, for everyday use there have always been chemical intoxicants. All the vegetable sedatives and narcotics, all the euphorics that grow on trees, the hallucinogens that ripen in berries or can be squeezed from roots—all, without exception, have been known and systematically used by human beings from time immemorial."

Huxley seems to have been close to the mark in his idea of the brain as a filter. Modern research has shown that two substances in the brain—serotonin and norepinephrine—act as switches that control the signals the cortex sends the brain. When the system's norepinephrine is increased or the serotonin reduced, the switches are changed so that the cortex is titillated and the brain is destabilized. Apparently LSD does in fact have this effect. The reduction filter is knocked out, and the brain is free to produce its own internal landscape of images—hallucinations.

Huxley was convinced of the good effects of his mescaline experience, although he did not equate it, or any other drug experience, with the true enlightenment that he, by then a practicing Buddhist, considered to be "the end and ultimate purpose of human life." But he believed drugs could assist toward that end, pharmacologically providing a spiritual state that Catholic theologians call "a gratuitous grace"—something that, though not necessary to salvation, may be helpful. "To be shaken out of the ruts of ordinary perception," wrote Huxley, "to be shown for a few timeless hours the outer and the inner world, not as they appear to an animal obsessed with survival or to a human being obsessed with words and notions, but as they are apprehended, directly and unconditionally, by Mind at Large—this is an experience of inestimable value to everyone."

Still, Huxley chose to tread lightly in extolling the potential benefits of mind-expanding drugs. He predicted—rightly, as it turned out—strong resistance to his ideas from the dominant Western culture, with its strongly rational foundations. Yet experimental research continued with the drugs, which came to be called psychedelics (an apt adaptation of Greek words meaning "mind made visible"), and other proselytes for chemical enlightenment were less circumspect than Huxley. One, a psychologist named Timothy Leary, eventually came to embody a revolutionary spirit of mental exploration.

Leary was a well-regarded—if somewhat flamboyant—teacher and researcher in 1958 when he resigned from his position as director of psychological research at the Kaiser Foundation Hospital in Oakland, California. Personally and professionally, Leary's life was in turmoil. Three years earlier, his disintegrating marriage had ended when his wife committed suicide; at the same time, he was trying to come to grips with the apparent failures of his chosen field. In ten years of keeping score, Leary and his staff had found that no matter what method they used, the patients they treated did about as well as those they did not—one-third got better, one-third got worse, and one-third stayed about the same.

Leaving California with a small research grant and some cash from insurance policies, Leary moved to Europe with his two children and spent a year "reading philosophy and thinking." The result was the manuscript of a book called *The Existential Transaction,* in which Leary suggested new means for changing behavior. He favored a humanist approach, with researchers learning about the mind by working with people in real-life situations, a method similar to that of a naturalist in the field. Rather than simply examining, diagnosing, and treating patients, he wanted psychologists to help them by emphasizing inner potential and change through self-reliance. To do so, practitioners would have to become involved with their subjects, he counseled, and be prepared "to change as much or more than the subjects being studied."

While living in Florence, Leary met David McClelland, the director of the Harvard Center for Personality Research, who was visiting Italy on a sabbatical leave. McClelland had read Leary's earlier work on psychotherapy and was impressed by it; after listening to his new ideas, the director offered him a job on the spot. Leary would teach a graduate seminar on psychotherapy.

Leary was a maverick from the day he arrived on the Harvard campus in Cambridge, Massachusetts. He complemented his professorial tweeds with white sneakers (he was later described by Albert Hofmann as looking more like a tennis champion than a Harvard lecturer) and engaged in endless late-night discussions with students over half-gallon jugs of California wine. He soon gathered around him a group of young scholars impatient with the established approaches to changing human nature—the best of which seemed far too slow. Leary had strong reservations, though, when one graduate student told him of experiments with the drug mescaline; Leary disapproved of such chemical meddling with the natural psyche.

That conservative attitude changed in the summer of 1960, however. Before he left for a vacation in Mexico, Leary talked with Frank Barron, a longtime California friend who would soon be coming to Harvard as a visiting professor. On a recent visit to Mexico, Barron had obtained some hallucinogenic "magic mushrooms" from a psychiatrist. The mystical insights and perspectives that Barron experienced after eating the fungi led him to believe they might be the instruments for behavioral change that he and Leary had often discussed. Leary remained skeptical, but when he was offered the chance to try some mushrooms in Mexico, he was quick to accept.

The mushrooms were bitter and stringy, with a smell that reminded Leary of a moldy New England basement. He gulped six, washing them down with beer, then sat back around a swimming pool with a group of friends to wait for the effects. Soon he began to feel strange: mildly nauseated, detached from his fellow mushroom eaters. Gradually the rest of the world, even inanimate objects, began quivering with life. Glancing at an abstaining friend who was taking notes, Leary burst into uproarious laughter as he realized that the watcher had no idea what he was observing. "I laughed again at my own everyday pomposity," Leary later wrote, "the narrow arrogance of scholars, the impudence of the rational, the smug naivete of words in contrast to the raw rich ever-changing panoramas that flooded my brain. . . . I gave way to delight, as mystics have for centuries when they peeked through the curtains and discovered that this world—so manifestly real—was actually a tiny stage set constructed by the mind. There was a sea of possibilities out there (in there?), other realities, an infinite array of programs for other futures."

The tropical liana plant (right), or ayahuasca, is one of the two plants Amazonian shamans combine in their potent hallucinogenic drink, also known as ayahuasca. In the painting below, the mixing of the ayahuasca and chacruna plants is depicted by the impending union of two snakes. To the left of the snakes, a shaman and his disciples sit around a pot of ayahuasca brew, enveloped in the energy of the vines. At right, smoking his snake-shaped pipe, stands the gardener who tends the ayahuasca plant. The skulls warn those who would partake of the potent brew without the proper knowledge and reverence.

Visions of a Hallucinogenic Jungle

Beyond ordinary reality and the boundaries of the everyday mind, say the Amazonian shamans, lies a world of spirit guides, sorcerers, magical illnesses, and magical cures. They reach this world with the help of a vision-inducing drug extracted from local plants. Mixed into a drink called ayahuasca and sipped in prescribed doses, the hallucinogen appears to open gates to other realms. Some say ayahuasca—also called the vine of death—is so powerful that its visions can kill a careless user with fear.

During fifteen years as a *vegetalista*—or "plant healer"—Peruvian painter Pablo Amaringo regularly drank aya-huasca. From the vivid mental images it produced, he claims to have learned how to cure illnesses and how to mix colors for his paintings. In 1975, threatened by shamans who envied his powers, Amaringo forsook his vegetalista practice and the potent ayahuasca. But he still recalled his visions clearly enough to paint them.

In 1985, visiting scholar Luis Eduardo Luna urged Amaringo to describe more of his visions on canvas and in words. The works shown here and on the following pages are taken from a book by the two called *Ayahuasca Visions: The Religious Iconography of Pablo Amaringo, a Peruvian Shaman.*

Like the colored arcs of a brilliant rainbow, the hierarchy of powers in the invisible world is revealed in Amaringo's painting. Starting with the green arc, containing animals and plants known to novice shamans, each band represents more transcendent knowledge. In the pinkish arc are hypnotic animals and fortunetellers; the blue arc holds angels with extrasensory powers; and in the violet arc are kings, queens, fairies, and muses. Tiny by comparison, the vegetalistas at lower left drink ayahuasca to learn about the array of powers. The circles around their hut symbolize icaros, magical songs that summon the visions.

Queen Pulsarium Coya grants four vegetalistas the power to diagnose patients by
"pulsing"—feeling their pulses. She has
also given them animal guardians, seen
clinging to their sleeves, who will help
the shamans identify various maladies.
The bands snaking across the painting
represent the healers' brain waves moving in synchrony with their patients'
pulsations; above the bands, the forest
teems with spirits associated with pulsing. At top right, above the bearded men,
hovers a UFO from a realm vegetalistas
are said to visit when using ayahuasca.

Good and evil face off in the dramatic painting below as a sorcerer and his bat-shaped evil spirit (upper left) prepare to attack a gathering of vegetalistas. In addition to the bat spirit, who is sending sonic waves to make his victims sleepy, the sorcerer's nefarious allies include evil fireflies, deadly house lizards, and red-necked sorcerer birds. The shaman, who is shown wearing a protective design on his back and spewing dazzling waves of color to blind his enemy, is also aided by an army of spirits, including a snake toad and the parrot snake (lower left), whose human arms hurl poisoned daggers.

Calling on their helping spirits, a master vegetalista and his two apprentices (above) use various healing methods. The master, kneeling over his patient, calls on his powerful white phlegm to extract magical darts from a woman's stomach. At center, an apprentice fans a woman with an achote plant to cure her of a fright caused by an evil spirit. A second apprentice sings over a love-struck man (seated) who has fallen ill because he used a love charm improperly. Aiding the apprentice are the spirits of the red goat, whose breath has curative powers, and a snake (top right) that will draw out the man's insanity.

Clutching pipes, three addicts drift into a drug-induced stupor in a turn-of-the-century opium den in New York's Chinatown. Smoked, eaten, or sipped as tea throughout history, opium is an addictive narcotic derived from the same poppy that yields morphine and heroin.

the drugs, he and his team could use them to explore the true essence of psychology, aesthetics, philosophy, religion—even life itself.

By the spring of 1961, Leary and fellow Harvard researcher Richard Alpert had administered psychedelic drugs to more than 200 subjects. They discovered a broad range of responses, not only in different subjects, but even during different occasions for the same subject. Leary and Alpert came to understand that these vagaries were determined by the dosage of the drug as well as by two variables they called "set" and "setting." Set refers to a person's expectations of the drug's effects, setting to the physical and social environment in which the drug is taken. By insisting on the importance of these variables, Leary and Alpert were able to isolate more accurately the real—as opposed to the subjective—effects of the drugs.

Despite the variety of experiences, a vast majority of the subjects reported positive reactions: 85 percent of them said the experience was the most educational of their lives. There was no way of demonstrating, however, that any of the subjects' lives were actually permanently improved, and Leary and Alpert looked for a situation that would provide an objective index. They found it in a nearby state prison, where they were invited to see if they could help inmates change the patterns of their lives. The first prison volunteers were an intimidating lot—two murderers, two armed robbers, an embezzler, and a

Leary's journey beyond the normal limits of his mind lasted about four hours, and he returned profoundly changed. He felt he had done more in this short trip to investigate the vast unexplored realms of the brain than he had in his fifteen previous years as a psychologist. Like Georgei Gurdjieff before him, he became convinced that the brain is underutilized and capable of being reprogrammed for greatly expanded intelligence and consciousness. Instead of Gurdjieff's exercises, though, Leary regarded psychedelic drugs as the key to achieving and analyzing these higher levels of awareness. As one researcher put it, the drugs would provide a "pharmacological bridge to transcendence."

Returning to Harvard, Leary established a research program to explore the matter further. He legally obtained a quantity of psilocybin, the active ingredient of the mushrooms, and worked out a plan of interactive participation in which his investigators took the drugs along with their subjects. Leary believed that once they learned to accurately chart the mind wanderings prompted by various doses of

Cocaine was the active ingredient of a "digestive tonic" promoted as a beauty secret in this late-1800s French poster. While it renders a euphoric state of mind, cocaine can also confer a powerful addiction, paranoid psychosis, and fatal convulsions.

COCA DES INCAS
VIN TONIQUE & DIGESTIF
DÉPÔT GÉNÉRAL - 26 - Rue de Pontoise - PARIS
IMPRIE
LA COMMERCIALE
17, Rue Martel
PARIS
Que faites-vous ma chère pour rester aussi belle?
Je bois chaque jour du COCA DES INCAS

heroin dealer—and Leary's work with them started off on the wrong foot. The setting of the cold, sunless penitentiary was depressing, and when Leary admitted his fear of the criminals, one inmate responded by describing his own counterproductive feeling, a fear of the "mad scientist." Suddenly laughter filled the room, and the session turned into an enlightening one for all the participants; the convicts experienced the same mind-opening phenomena that the graduate students had.

In the program's second year, the convicts appeared to benefit from their insights: They perceived new possibilities for life outside of prison and were given considerable emotional support in the parole period by the Harvard project coordinators. Many succeeded on their new paths; within a year of release, only about 10 percent of those paroled wound up in prison again, whereas 70 percent of their untreated peers returned to jail.

While the prison project continued in 1962, Leary took part in another, radically different study. Collaborating with Walter Pahnke, a young medical doctor studying religion, he set up an experiment to test the effect of psilocybin on the intensity of the mystical and religious experience. The session took place on Good Friday in the chapel of Boston University, with twenty carefully briefed theology students as subjects. Half of the students were given the drug, and the other half took a dummy pill; none were told which they had taken. All listened to a long religious service with organ and vocal music, readings, prayers, and personal meditation. Pahnke collected data from the participants for six months and discovered distinct differences between the two test groups. He checked the subjects' description of their experience on that Good Friday against a list of sensations that had been recounted by mystics in other circum-

stances, such as ineffability—the failure of words to express the experience—and a sense of transcendence of time and space. On every count, those who took psilocybin showed far greater intensity of religious experience than those in the control group; fully half of the drug takers reported lasting positive changes in their attitudes and behavior as a result of the Good Friday session.

These encouraging results convinced Leary and Alpert that psychedelic drugs could play a key role in transforming society. They wrote a manual for their mystical undertakings entitled *The Psychedelic Journey*, choosing as their model the *Bardo Thodol*, or Tibetan *Book of the Dead*. This great Buddhist text, aimed at the living, spells out all the levels of consciousness leading up to the "clear light of illumination," a transcendent state of liberation from the ego. Leary showed the parallels between these levels and the altered states induced by psychedelic drugs, and he hopefully predicted that one way his scientific drug program could work for the good of society was by helping people explore the sacred realms of the mind.

Leary soon learned, however, that society did not want to be transformed. His drug-tinted panacea was poison to the establishment. Influential members of the Harvard faculty were alienated by the project's flamboyantly rebellious image and by Leary's own high profile as a promoter of the new consciousness. There was also trouble with the administration at the university; deans were fielding many complaints from parents whose children phoned home to announce that they had discovered the secret of the universe.

It made little difference that these undergraduates were not part of Leary's project, which involved only grad-

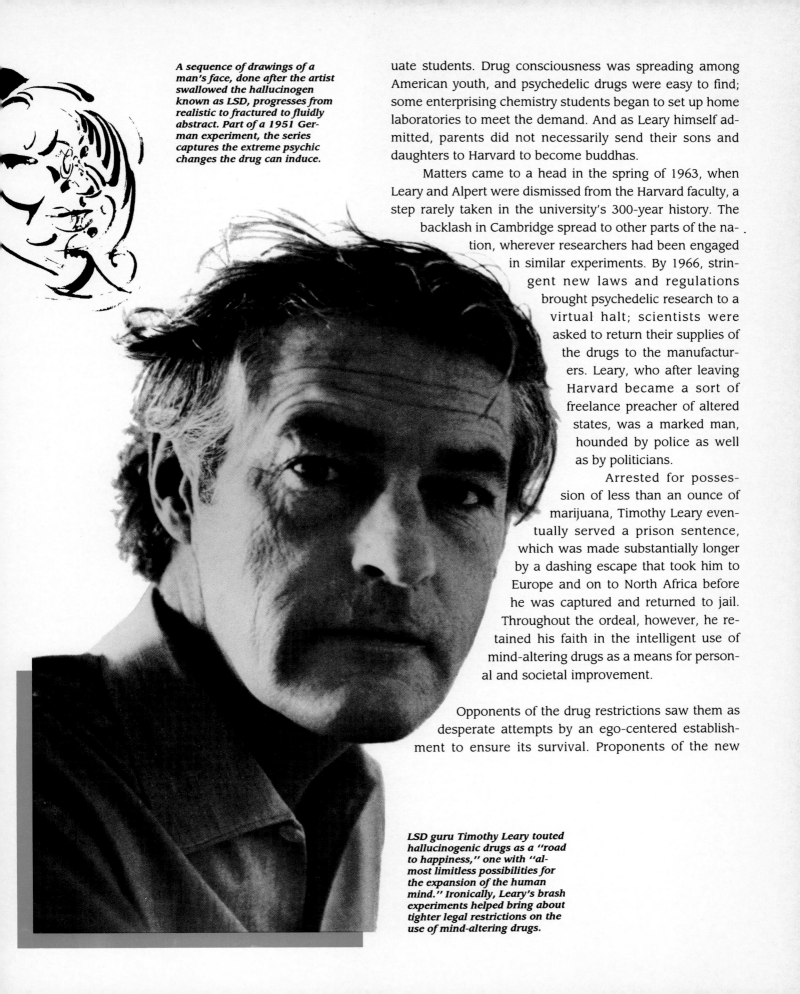

A sequence of drawings of a man's face, done after the artist swallowed the hallucinogen known as LSD, progresses from realistic to fractured to fluidly abstract. Part of a 1951 German experiment, the series captures the extreme psychic changes the drug can induce.

uate students. Drug consciousness was spreading among American youth, and psychedelic drugs were easy to find; some enterprising chemistry students began to set up home laboratories to meet the demand. And as Leary himself admitted, parents did not necessarily send their sons and daughters to Harvard to become buddhas.

Matters came to a head in the spring of 1963, when Leary and Alpert were dismissed from the Harvard faculty, a step rarely taken in the university's 300-year history. The backlash in Cambridge spread to other parts of the nation, wherever researchers had been engaged in similar experiments. By 1966, stringent new laws and regulations brought psychedelic research to a virtual halt; scientists were asked to return their supplies of the drugs to the manufacturers. Leary, who after leaving Harvard became a sort of freelance preacher of altered states, was a marked man, hounded by police as well as by politicians.

Arrested for possession of less than an ounce of marijuana, Timothy Leary eventually served a prison sentence, which was made substantially longer by a dashing escape that took him to Europe and on to North Africa before he was captured and returned to jail. Throughout the ordeal, however, he retained his faith in the intelligent use of mind-altering drugs as a means for personal and societal improvement.

Opponents of the drug restrictions saw them as desperate attempts by an ego-centered establishment to ensure its survival. Proponents of the new

LSD guru Timothy Leary touted hallucinogenic drugs as a "road to happiness," one with "almost limitless possibilities for the expansion of the human mind." Ironically, Leary's brash experiments helped bring about tighter legal restrictions on the use of mind-altering drugs.

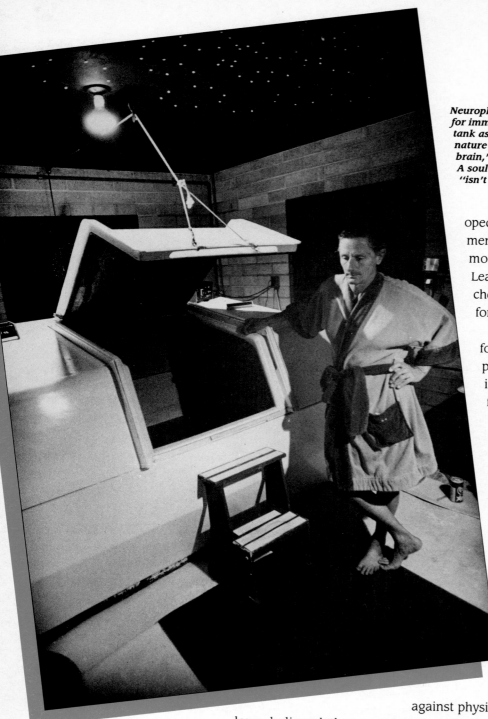

Neurophysiologist John Lilly prepares for immersion in a sensory-deprivation tank as part of his research into the nature of the mind. "We are not the brain," he asserts, and "not the body. A soul essence inhabits us," which "isn't tied to brain activity at all."

oped during the 1960s, LSD maintained the sacramental status that Leary had ascribed to it. Furthermore, like the prisoners and theology students Leary treated with the drug, many felt that the psychedelic experience profoundly changed their lives for the better.

Despite the dire warnings of the anti-LSD forces, very little solid evidence has emerged to prove that psychedelic drugs typically cause lasting damage, either physical or psychic. Although flashbacks (recurrences of LSD's effects), chronic anxiety states, and schizophrenia-like psychoses sometimes occur after frequent exposure to the drug, the questions of brain cell or chromosome damage have not yet been satisfactorily answered on a scientific basis. In fact, according to scientists who stoutly defend their drug-related research, mind-altering substances such as LSD, to say nothing of the nonhallucinogenic marijuana, are positively benign compared with those much more dangerous drugs of choice, alcohol and tobacco.

Still, anyone in an altered state of consciousness is also in a vulnerable state, whatever means were used to reach that condition. The normal defenses against physical and psychic dangers are relaxed, and dangerous—sometimes tragic—situations arise. Converts at religious revival meetings, in an ecstatic longing to be reborn, have thrown themselves into rivers and drowned; innumerable cases of "possession" tell of victims who inflicted wounds on themselves or others while in the grip of an alternate personality; sleepwalkers have sauntered along perilously high balconies. Leary tells of an episode in the early days of his experimental work with LSD in which a subject took the drug even though both the set and the setting were negative. The subject spent the next several hours bounding around like a gorilla, climbing drainpipes and swinging in

laws believed that psychedelics were dangerous drugs that should be administered only by physicians in a medical setting. The prohibitionists had a point: As Leary and Alpert had learned in their investigation of set and setting, psychedelics could unleash powerful negative reactions in people who were ill prepared for the experience or who took the drugs in hostile environments.

Nevertheless, the drug ban had little effect on the rising tide of personal experimentation with psychedelics. For many youths in the substantial counterculture that devel-

trees, covering himself with cuts and bruises. It was one of the first ''bad trips'' that Leary witnessed, and it convinced him that strict controls over the set and setting of experiments, as well as over the purity of the drugs, must always be maintained.

But there was yet another problem with using psychedelics as a key to revelation. Even those who defend the use of drugs as a tool for positive mind expansion have had to admit that the glorious effects of drug-induced consciousness altering are all too often temporary. Again and again the exhilarating revelations of a drug experience have faded with the light of dawn. As philosopher and author Arthur Koestler put it in 1960, after trying psilocybin with Leary in Cambridge, ''I solved the secret of the universe last night, but this morning I forgot what it was.''

So, pressured by antidrug laws and disillusioned by the ephemeral effects of their magic pills, devotees began to look for other methods of pursuing their spiritual goals. Many turned back to the meditative practices of Eastern religions. Like Aldous Huxley before them, they found that the highs reached by meditation were purer and longer lasting than those obtained through drugs. Meditation is also devoid of the physical side effects of drugs, such as dilated eyes, cold hands, nausea, and wakefulness, which have nothing to do with the desired mental state.

Furthermore, while drugs seemed to reveal new dimensions of the mind, they also reinforced the illusion that those dimensions were accessible only by external, material means. Mystics—and some drug researchers—believe that those dimensions are actually available to anyone, anytime, even though most people do not know how to reach them without drugs. The goal of meditation is to overcome illusion and to know that higher levels of consciousness come from the mind itself.

Richard Alpert discovered the power of meditative highs when he traveled to India in 1967 to find out how Eastern holy men reacted to psychedelics. In the foothills of the Himalayas he displayed his treasured stock of LSD to yoga master Neem Karoli Baba—who promptly consumed it

all. The astonished Alpert saw no effect whatsoever on the holy man from the drug, enough for dozens of ordinary psychedelic excursions. When someone explained that the holy man operated at a level of consciousness that did not depend on physical or biological stimulation, Alpert realized he had come upon a spiritual source well beyond his previous experience.

Alpert stayed in India for a year, living in a small hut, bathing each morning in the icy water of a mountain stream, and filling his days with yoga exercises assigned by the guru. Returning to the United States as Baba Ram Dass, he became a popular lecturer and author, communicating the wisdom of the East to Western audiences.

Those audiences included more than the veterans of the psychedelic revolution. Many people who had never used drugs were also eager to find a safe way to explore the outer reaches of their minds. Not everyone, however, was prepared to take Alpert's ascetic route to transformation; many were put off by the persistence and effort required to expand their consciousness through meditation. There remained a demand for mind-altering methods with the power and immediacy of drugs but without their dangers, and by the end of the 1960s, more typically American paths to higher consciousness were beginning to emerge.

John Lilly was a leading figure in this movement to map inner space. Trained as a medical doctor, he performed research in fields as diverse as biophysics, neurophysiology, electronics, and neuroanatomy. Lilly also garnered substantial fame for his work on relations between humans and dolphins, fictionalized on film in 1973's *The Day of the Dolphin.* His interest in dolphins grew from an experiment he conducted in 1954, while working at the National Institute for Mental Health near Washington, D.C. To test a then-current theory that people remain awake only if they are continuously bombarded by sensory stimuli, Lilly decided to put himself in an environment with the minimum possible sensory input. He found a water tank in a small, soundproof room that he filled with water at 93 degrees Fahrenheit—the temperature at which

Resplendently garbed, Telsen-Sao leader Jeshahr the Guide (left) exudes a cosmic authority that transcends his earlier careers as dishwasher and bank employee. His sleeve insignia, the winged lion of San Marco, represents peaceful intent—a key to safe out-of-body travel.

A School for Astral Travelers

I found myself in an indefinable sphere of feelings and music. Every image became small like the head of a pin and then split into an endless number of visions, sometimes like paradise, sometimes monstrous. The shadows of a thousand hands tried to catch me, but I was flying very fast." Thus did a young man called Nirvan describe the curious mental journey he undertook in 1988 at Telsen-Sao, a quasi-military school in Italy devoted to the training of out-of-body travelers.

Throughout the ages, a few sensitive people have said their consciousness could at times slip away in an insubstantial "astral body," a weightless form capable of flying off at great speeds and then returning to the physical body. But those who run Telsen-Sao (an Italian acronym for "extrasensory learning") claim to have transformed that personal phenomenon into an ability attainable through proper instruction and rigid discipline—an assertion apparently accepted by students, despite uniforms and equipment that lend the institution an air of a low-budget 1950s sci-fi thriller.

Telsen-Sao cadets study such topics as cosmic navigation, geography, and a supposedly universal language called Jeshaele. That preparation is potentially lifesaving, says the school's founder, Renato Minozzi, now known as Jeshahr the Guide. Claiming to have first left his own body during a 1971 coma, Jeshahr believes that untrained astral travelers risk becoming forever lost in "other spheres"—such as the realms of the dead and the immortal. At last report, no cadets had failed to return from a mission.

Under a glowing ankhlike emblem that combines a cross, a crescent, and a star of David, students in the Celestial Abyss course plot their astral flight paths. Telsen-Sao navigation methods involve sound, color, radio waves, and a complex pyramidal coordinate system.

"Ground to Pilot: Maintain Your Course!"

Like the crew of a large military aircraft, a Telsen-Sao astral travel team includes both a pilot and a navigator. And as the journey begins, a guide comparable to an air-traffic controller offers flight instructions that only the initiated know how to apply: "Rudder completely up. Correct six degrees to the right. Good, proceed."

According to Jeshahr, the pilot alone embarks on the actual out-of-body experience. The navigator remains behind, serving as a communications link between pilot and guide and, in theory, supplementing the pilot's efforts with extra psychic power. Even with that assistance, pilots are reportedly so quickly exhausted that school policy limits all flights to no more than twenty-eight minutes.

On cots in Telsen-Sao's "astro-dynamic laboratory," two cadets wearing copper breastplates said to draw on their electromagnetic fields start an astral journey. As the pilot (below, left) separates mind and body, the navigator (right) is said to provide a boost of "lymph energy" through electric circuits linking the cadets.

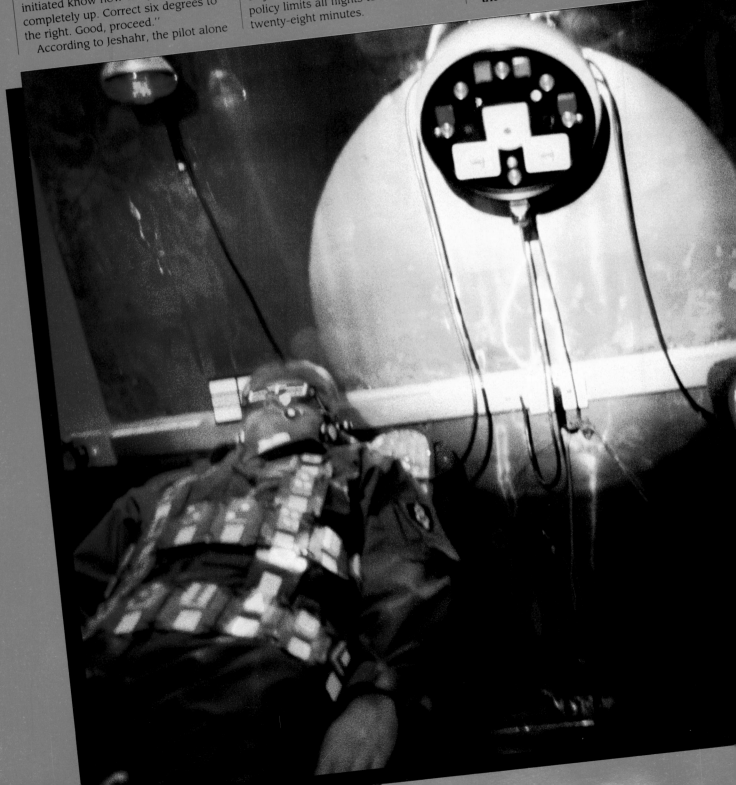

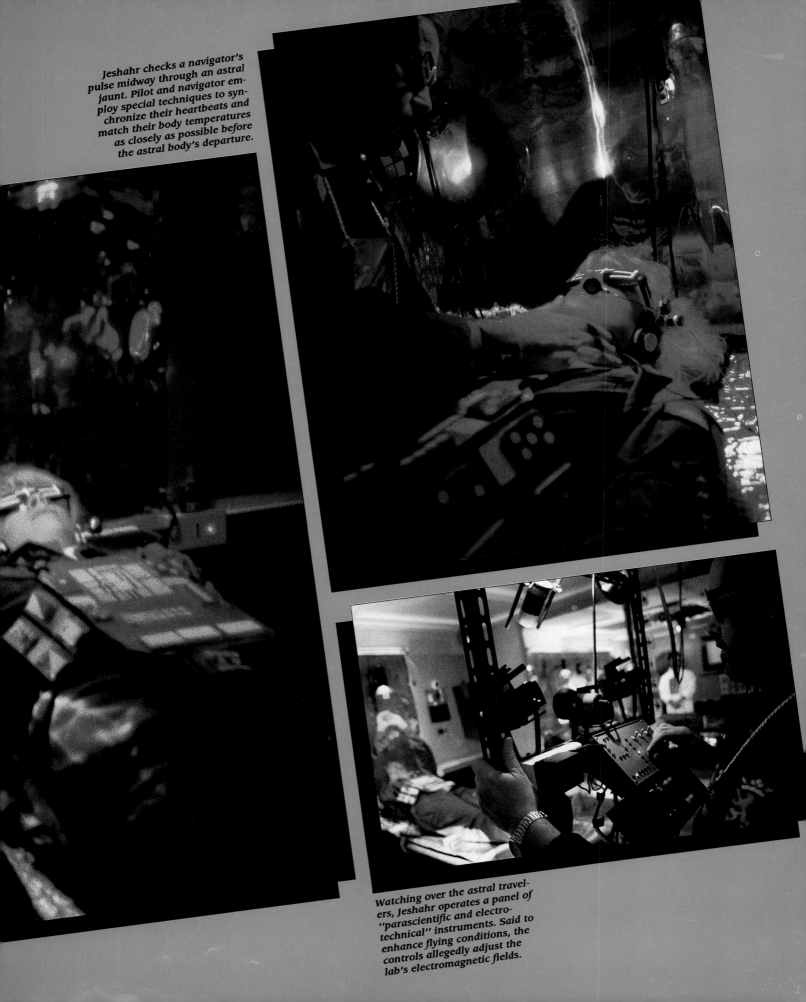

Jeshahr checks a navigator's pulse midway through an astral jaunt. Pilot and navigator employ special techniques to synchronize their heartbeats and match their body temperatures as closely as possible before the astral body's departure.

Watching over the astral travelers, Jeshahr operates a panel of "parascientific and electro-technical" instruments. Said to enhance flying conditions, the controls allegedly adjust the lab's electromagnetic fields.

the human body feels neither hot nor cold. Wearing a special breathing apparatus, Lilly climbed naked into the tank to float in the seemingly gravity-free darkness.

Later versions of the apparatus came to be called sensory-deprivation tanks, but Lilly reported no deprivation. In fact, he found that the absence of external stimulation quickly gave rise to heightened inner awareness; he reported experiencing trances, dreams, mystical visions, and out-of-body travels. He concluded that when sensory input was removed, the brain—which he dubbed a "biocomputer"—released its own program of sensory experiences, limited only by one's imagination.

To Lilly, a trip in the tank was liberating; he could choose programs that took him to various transcendent states of consciousness. "There you are suspended in an embryonic silence," he later wrote, "and suddenly the Logos, the Universal Vibration, begins to pervade the fabric of awareness, coming at once from inside and all directions."

Floating in the waters at NIMH, John Lilly began to wonder what it would be like to be buoyant all the time, a line of thought that led him to work with dolphins. Even as he searched for—and found—various ways to communicate with the large-brained sea mammals, however, Lilly maintained his newfound interest in mystical reality. In the early 1960s, he took LSD for the first time and began a new set of explorations.

Realizing that his scientific training gave him little background for interpreting his experiences, Lilly sought out philosophers, psychologists, and mystics to consult and compare notes. He worked on maps of uncharted levels of consciousness, correlating them with the states described by Gurdjieff and the Eastern mystics. Lilly also began to write popular books about the power of his discoveries, and he urged others to seek higher states of consciousness. In a 1972 book called *The Center of the Cyclone,* he asserted that if everyone on the planet regularly reached higher levels of awareness, problems such as pollution, famine, disease, and war would soon be solved through rational means. Lilly also affirmed that such consciousness raising could bring

immediate benefits on a smaller scale: "A corporation that encourages its management and its labor to achieve basic and higher levels of consciousness can show increasing efficiency, harmony, productivity, improved policies and better public relations within a few months. . . . The higher states of consciousness and the means of reaching them are an economic asset worth more money than one can currently measure."

The corporate world did not beat a path to Lilly's door, but he was not alone in his call to enhance institutional harmony—indeed to transform society itself—through concerted consciousness raising. Maharishi Mahesh Yogi, who preaches to a worldwide following from headquarters in Holland, teaches a form of mind expansion known as Transcendental Meditation—TM, for short. Like Lilly, the guru insists that the hope of a new world order lies in altered states of mind.

The guru's disciples point to an experiment in which some 11,000 inmates of prisons in Senegal were taught the TM program. Within a week, it is claimed, a dramatic improvement in the prison atmosphere was evident. Eventually, authorities reported a 70 to 80 percent drop in medical consultations and, most wondrous of all, an 85 percent drop in recidivism among released prisoners. On a grander scale, followers of the maharishi claim evidence to prove that when enough devotees practice TM in one place, the whole world's tensions and ills are reduced: Angry nations become less belligerent, sickness decreases, oil prices decline, and stock prices rise. On the strength of these claims, the maharishi has called for governments to fund a perpetual body of 7,000 TM disciples who, he insists, can create a "wave of coherence and harmony" that will decisively alleviate the world's afflictions and advance the goal of "bringing heaven on Earth for all mankind on a permanent basis."

The guru's grand scheme may never find a backer, but the idea of applying mind-altering techniques to achieve tangible benefits has held particular appeal for Americans, raised in a culture with a strong ethos of self-help. A typical

Maharishi Mahesh Yogi arrives in London from his native India in 1961, near the start of a ten-year mission to the West. The guru won popularity with his drug-free prescription for happiness and mind expansion through meditation. "Turning the attention inward," he taught, would put the conscious mind "in contact with the creative intelligence that gives rise to every thought."

early prophet of personal transformation was Napoleon Hill, author of the 1937 book *Think and Grow Rich*. The way to a life of harmony and prosperity, Hill believed, was through the subconscious mind. He taught a form of self-hypnosis called autosuggestion, by which a person could nourish the subconscious with "thoughts of a creative nature." Hill excited many followers with the promise that dramatic accomplishment awaited those who could envision themselves "on the road to success."

Those who carried Hill's self-help philosophy into the 1970s and 1980s were more sophisticated, tying their messages to lessons imported from Western science and Eastern religion. Best-selling American author Shakti Gawain propounded a technique called creative visualization: If a person could create a clear image of something desirable, then continue to focus on that image regularly, it would eventually become a reality. The goal might be physical—a new home or job, for example—or it might be improvement at an emotional, mental, or spiritual level. Creating and nurturing the internal experience, according to Gawain, will give rise to the external experience as well.

To explain the phenomenon, Gawain turned to modern physics. Matter, when viewed at atomic and subatomic levels, can be understood either as an aggregation of tiny particles or as a network of intertwined fields of energy. Because thought, too, is energy, Gawain avers, it can interact with the energy that makes up matter. Holding a clear idea firmly in the mind can "attract and create that form on the material plane," even without any direct action.

Along with such scientific-sounding descriptions of creative visualization, Gawain reinforces her position with assertions of a more mystical nature. She exhorts her readers, for example, to believe that "we are all in essence perfect, spiritual beings," and she suggests that by changing our innermost beliefs "we can eliminate illness and disease altogether." At a more practical level, Gawain and other proponents of creative visualization rely on techniques derived from the meditative practices of the East. Complete physical relaxation is the first step, combined with deep, slow, regular breathing. The visualization itself requires intense concentration on the desired image, in the way that a Buddhist monk, meditating on a holy phrase, repeats it over and over.

Visualization techniques lend

The mind's powers to heal the body, overcome hardship, and reach new levels of awareness pervade the teachings of these four distinguished Americans. Mary Baker Eddy (top left) founded the Christian Science movement in 1876 after healing her own illnesses through Bible reading and prayer. Famed minister Norman Vincent Peale (top right), in his book entitled The Power of Positive Thinking, taught that with belief in oneself and in God, anyone can "conquer personal fear, triumph over adversity, and transform and enhance daily life."

Shakti Gawain (bottom left), whose Hindu first name means "energy," advocates "creative visualization" as a means of bringing goals into sharp focus and then realizing them. Journalist and educator Norman Cousins (bottom right) found that medical treatment is far more effective if bolstered by "hope, faith, love, will to live, purpose, laughter, and festivity." During his long and painful illness, to which he succumbed in 1991, Cousins said that "ten minutes of solid belly laughter would give me two hours of pain-free sleep."

themselves to many applications, from healthcare to sports. Some doctors teach patients to visualize their immune systems fighting off illness, thus empowering their natural defenses against disease. A cancer patient, for example, might imagine a tumor as a vicious animal surrounded by millions of white dogs—white blood cells—tearing it to pieces and devouring it. Some reports indicate that such visualizations may play a fundamental role in relieving symptoms and even in achieving cures.

Athletes frequently use visualization systems to achieve peak performance. Relaxed and removed from competitive pressure, an athlete imagines a specific action, such as a tennis stroke or a basketball shot, and repeats it over and over, mentally correcting for any errors. Studies show that mental "practice" for specific athletic skills can be as effective as physical drills, particularly if the visualizer can make real in his or her mind the sensory details of the drill—such as feeling a ball in the hands or hearing it bounce on the floor. Champion golfer Ben Hogan made it a habit to mentally rehearse each shot, trying to "feel" the club head meeting the ball and his club following through. Many other amateur and professional athletes, including Soviet Olympic competitors, make visualization a key element of their practice regimens.

One commercial mental-training program goes beyond simple visualization. In addition to supplying other teaching materials, it provides athletes with videotapes of an expert demonstrating skills over and over. The movement is shown at normal speed and in slow motion, and it is sometimes broken down into computerized graphics to illustrate the underlying mechanics. Music that accompanies the visuals accentuates the ideal tempo, rhythm, and timing of an optimal performance. After watching a tape, athletes are told to imagine performing each movement ten times in slow motion; regular repetition is said to promote the development of a "fluid and graceful rhythm" that parallels the skilled movement on the tape.

Visualization is only one of many learning techniques that seek to harness nonconscious levels of the mind. Research conducted in the early twentieth century indicated that people learned some things faster when training was supplemented with sleep learning. The instructional period for sailors learning Morse code, for instance, was reduced by three weeks when additional training was given during the sleeping hours. (Later research showed that the learning probably occurred when the trainees were not truly asleep but in a near-sleep state caused by the teaching itself.)

Newer learning systems take advantage of other states of consciousness that seem to share the heightened suggestibility of near sleep. Bulgarian psychiatrist Georgi Lozanov, after studying sleep learning and yoga, devised a technique that combines relaxation, repetition, and music to speed up learning of foreign languages. Music is a key ingredient. Lozanov's early research showed, not surprisingly, that when relaxed students tried to focus on learning, the stress of concentrating destroyed their relaxation. Then Lozanov found that when he played certain music—baroque orchestral pieces at a tempo of sixty beats per minute, to be exact—his subjects remained relaxed even while doing strenuous mental work. In some extraordinary all-day sessions under these conditions, his students were able to learn and retain more than 1,000 words of a foreign language, or nearly half of an everyday vocabulary.

All attempts at exploring and expanding the mind's potential notwithstanding, some theorists believe the next step for the human mind is to enter into a symbiosis with computers, actually moving human consciousness into more powerful, longer-lived machines. Subscribers to this idea cite the phenomenal development of computers in the last few decades, which has forced a reassessment of the meaning of the word *mind*. As the machines become faster and more capable, it gets harder and harder to tell if they are actually thinking, and a debate rages over whether machines can indeed become conscious.

In the most popular scenarios, the computers of today are merely ungainly precursors of wizard machines capable of a new kind of intelligence called post-biological, meaning that it does not spring directly from the human brain. This post-biological competence, also known as artificial intelligence, or AI, would eventually surpass human capabilities—all essential human functions would be matched by artificial counterparts. Machines would develop the ability to mastermind their own maintenance, reproduction, and improvement. The result would be intelligent robots, machines that would act and think like humans even if they bore little physical or mental resemblance.

The most sanguine AI champions foresee the emergence of a hybrid that combines the wisdom of the human mind with the power of the machine. Because the brain evolves so slowly, they say, humans' avid desire for greater knowledge and understanding can be met only by joining forces with computers. Some even imagine the most intimate union of these disparate minds—human and machine—in a phenomenon called transmigration. Since an ongoing computation can be halted in mid-process and transferred to a different computer, the argument goes, it follows that someday the memories and thought patterns within a human brain could be translated into computer language and moved over to a machine. One scenario has this transference happening piecemeal, with the human subject's brain being replaced section by section with computer units, until the flesh and blood organ is superseded altogether. Thus freed of its biological limitations, the human mind could experience in the material world the immortality it has always sought on the spiritual plane.

If the prospect of mechanical transcendence delights its advocates, it leaves others appalled. They see the specter of a future with computers in control, while the biological intelligence that created them dwindles in importance. Indeed, the computer era has given rise to numerous films, stories, and books that paint bleak pictures of machine-dominated futures. Before there can be any real understanding of future relations between humans and computers, however, a seemingly simple question must be

Aircraft Controlled by Thought Alone

Far from Hollywood, where screenwriters and special-effects experts have been staging such scenes for years, air force researchers are testing a highly advanced and imaginative set of aircraft controls. Unlike a steering stick, which requires touch to execute a maneuver, these new controls are operated by thought—or, more precisely, by brain waves, as represented in the composite photograph at right. So far, the system is earthbound, used only with a flight simulator in a laboratory at Wright-Patterson Air Force Base, near Dayton, Ohio. But some observers consider it a preview of the future.

The mind-driven controls are deceptively simple. Two fluorescent lights on the control panel flash on and off thirteen times a second, causing neurons in the pilot's visual cortex to fire at that frequency. Electrodes attached to the pilot's scalp relay his brain waves to a system that picks out the wave spiking thirteen times per second and measures it. The strength of that wave is displayed on the control panel. To maneuver the simulator, the flier consciously changes the strength of the brain wave. Suppressing it makes the simulator bank to the left; increasing the wave makes the simulator bank right; keeping the mind unengaged—but alert—holds the simulator level.

Not even Captain David Tumey, who heads the research project, can explain how people control their brain waves. "Some say that singing in your head raises the power," he offers, but other fliers just watch the bar scale as it registers change. They find the biofeedback-based system works remarkably well.

Tumey and his colleagues downplay the notion of pilots' one day roaring through dogfights on brain waves alone. For now, they want to know what stimulates brain waves, how they are related to thought, and how the waves differ from one person to the next. Nonetheless, the technology might help scientists determine how much information and how many tasks a pilot's brain can handle under stress—and how a computer might take on the overload.

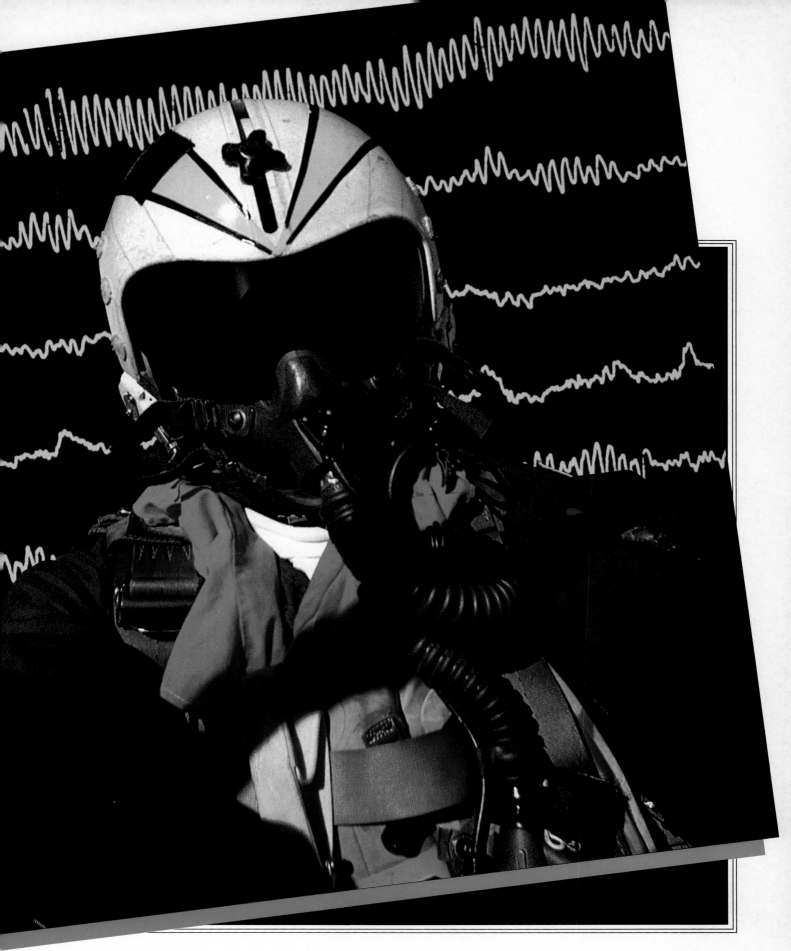

addressed: Can a machine duplicate the human mind?

The question, of course, brings to full circle the still unsolved problem of finding a satisfactory definition of mind. But one way to narrow the matter down is to ask if the computer can think. Alan Turing, a British mathematician who played a central role in the development of the first digital computers, was convinced that thought is essentially computational, and therefore something machines can do. In 1950, he proposed a classic test of the issue. Turing envisioned a human being in a room with a teletype machine. The person is not told whether the questions he or she sends via the teletype are being answered by another human or by a computer. If a computer is responding to the questions, said Turing, and if the person cannot tell whether the answers come from a human or from a computer, then it must be conceded that the computer can think.

One computer, created in the 1970s by AI researcher Kenneth Colby, succeeded in convincing a number of learned observers that it was human. The computer was programmed to imitate a person with paranoid tendencies and would sidestep questions it could not answer with agitated responses, such as "Maybe you have to watch out for the Mafia." After exchanging messages with the machine by teletype, several psychiatrists concluded that they were indeed conversing with someone whose powers of reasoning were somewhat impaired.

Even if they have not actually passed what is called the Turing test, some modern computers in a sense meet Turing's qualifications, at least in specialized tasks. A computer programmed to diagnose blood diseases, for example, can perform as well as any doctor. A chess-playing program can match skills with world-class players, while a backgammon program can beat them. Experts in AI predict that only time is needed to develop machines that will match the performance of human intelligence in every field. They make the analogy that if the sophisticated thinking machine of the future—the hardware—is compared to the brain, then the programs—software—that control the subtle interplay of electronic patterns correspond to the mind. Some people actually suggest that if such a combination of hardware and software could do everything a human mind could do, then we would have to concede that it possessed consciousness and that it experienced thoughts, even feelings.

The idea of an artificial mind with thought, consciousness, and a variety of mental states runs counter to the common conviction that mental states are uniquely human attributes—not material, but spiritual. Many thinkers argue fiercely against the AI prognosis of mechanical consciousness. The brain-to-mind relationship, they say, is not equivalent to the rule-bound combination of computer and programs. The way thoughts emerge in the brain can never be described by a formal set of rules, or algorithms, of the sort needed to construct a computer program.

In fact, goes one powerful anti-AI argument, no computational process can ever explain subjectivity. If consciousness were simply a matter of computation, then a pocket calculator would be conscious. But a calculator can only compute; it cannot think about what it is working on or be subjective about what it is doing. To put it another way, the calculator only does what it is doing; the mind knows what it is doing. And since the human brain does not know how it knows what it knows—does not, that is, know the source of its own consciousness—there is no way it could build a machine that "knows."

Thus even the effort to build an artificial mind leads back to questions about the nature and source of human consciousness—the same questions pursued so long and ardently by philosophers and psychologists, mushroom eaters and mystics. And the answers to those questions are still being sought, both by explorers who deliberately venture outside the limits of the ordinary mind to probe the hidden domains that lie beyond and by orthodox exponents of scientific objectivity. Whether answers exist or not, the wonder of the quest for them is aptly captured in the words of explorer John Lilly: "The miracle is that the universe created a part of itself to study the rest of it, that this part, in studying itself, finds the rest of the universe in its own natural inner realities."

Strange New Universe

A surgeon in search of a tumor walks into a patient's brain, passing like magic through folds of gray matter. A tourist picnics on the moon. Enveloped in a steamy Mesozoic forest, awed schoolchildren watch a fierce tyrannosaur stalk his prey. However much these notions may read like science fiction, they are among very real possibilities opened up by a fast-growing technology called virtual reality.

"For humans to make their next leap in civilization," says Thomas Furness, an expert in the field, "I believe we have to combine the machine and human intellects." Virtual reality—also called "cyberspace" or "telepresence"—does exactly that. With sophisticated computer graphics, it creates astonishing artificial landscapes or translates real but inaccessible environments—the interior of a live human organ as revealed by a CAT scan, say—into worlds the user can enter and explore. By means of feedback systems and sensors that monitor body movements, the participant's mind is immersed in the machine-created realm and is voluntarily deceived into responding to it as if it were real.

"Virtual reality eliminates the separation between you and the computer," explains one virtual explorer. "You are within it." Some who speculate on the future of this strange new technology foresee a day when an air-traffic controller may reach out and touch a three-dimensional image of a moving aircraft to guide it to safety—or a time when people will be able to create and enter their own dream worlds.

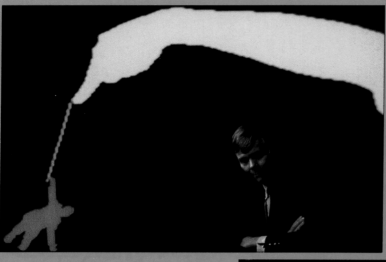

Myron Krueger displays one of his more whimsical virtual-reality programs. Behind him, a small computer-generated figure dangles and jumps on the end of a virtual string, responding appropriately to movements of the enormously enlarged virtual arm and hand of the person demonstrating the program. "Pressing buttons, pushing levers, and turning knobs is not the stuff from which adventures are made," says Krueger. "One would prefer to step into the graphic world unencumbered and be able to move around freely within it."

Explorers of the Virtual Unknown

Myron Krueger was among the first to pioneer the idea of stepping into a computer-created world. In the 1970s he developed a system known as Videoplace, which projects a moving camera image of the participant onto a graphic scene. The impression of being absorbed into an artificial world is so convincing, Krueger reports, that people instinctively touch themselves to make certain they are still here.

Jaron Lanier, founder of Virtual Programming Languages, Inc., in California, discovered a different means of entering virtual reality. Lanier has developed "computer clothing," including an elaborate headpiece called an EyePhone. "The goggles put a small TV in front of each eye so you see moving images in three dimensions," he explains. "The goggles have a sensor to tell where your head is facing. What you see is created completely by the computer." A DataGlove, with sensors that register finger movements, completes the outfit. "If you hold your hand in front of your face, you see a computer-generated hand in the virtual world," says Lanier. "If you wiggle your fingers, you see its fingers wiggle." With the glove, a user can pick up a virtual ball and throw it.

"Sometimes I think we've uncovered a new planet," Lanier says, "one that we're inventing instead of discovering. We're just starting to sight the shore of one of its continents. Virtual reality is an adventure worth centuries."

Wearing his DataGlove and ready to don his EyePhone (at left in picture below), Jaron Lanier prepares to enter his virtual environment. Lanier, who believes that virtual technology is destined to become a powerful teaching tool, has illustrated its effectiveness by teaching himself how to juggle within his artificial world. ''You learn to juggle in virtual reality by slowing down time and juggling with really slow balls,'' Lanier explains. ''And then you gradually speed it up until it's the same speed as the real world.''

Walk-In Blueprints and Brain Scans

Adventurous souls in various professions have already begun to put virtual reality to work. By translating blueprints into a visual structure, two architects tested the design of a proposed day-care center, moving through the rooms of a building that did not yet exist. Moreover, they virtually shrank themselves so they could view the center from a child's perspective. And a project at the San Diego Supercomputer Center enabled doctors to take a tour of a gigantic human brain. Physicians of the future may get a closeup look at problems by crawling around inside large virtual models of patients' bodies—created with input from modern scanning techniques such as computer axial tomography (CAT) and magnetic resonance imaging (MRI).

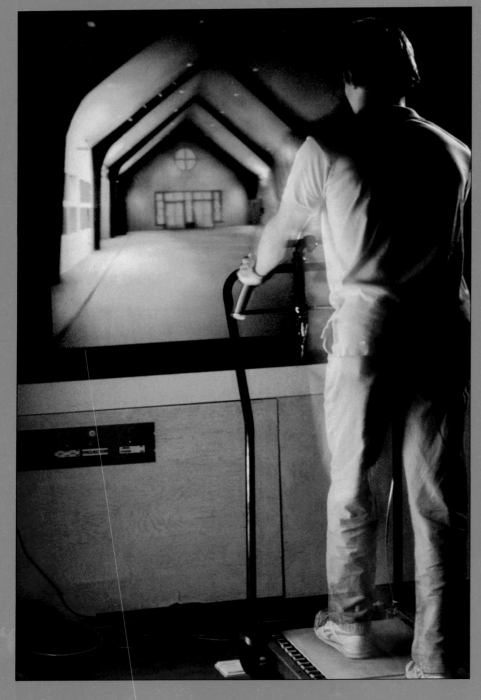

Using a computerized treadmill and a "magic helmet," an experimenter at the University of North Carolina (left) tours a building that has not been built. Through virtual reality, one architect discovered and corrected a design flaw before actual construction began.

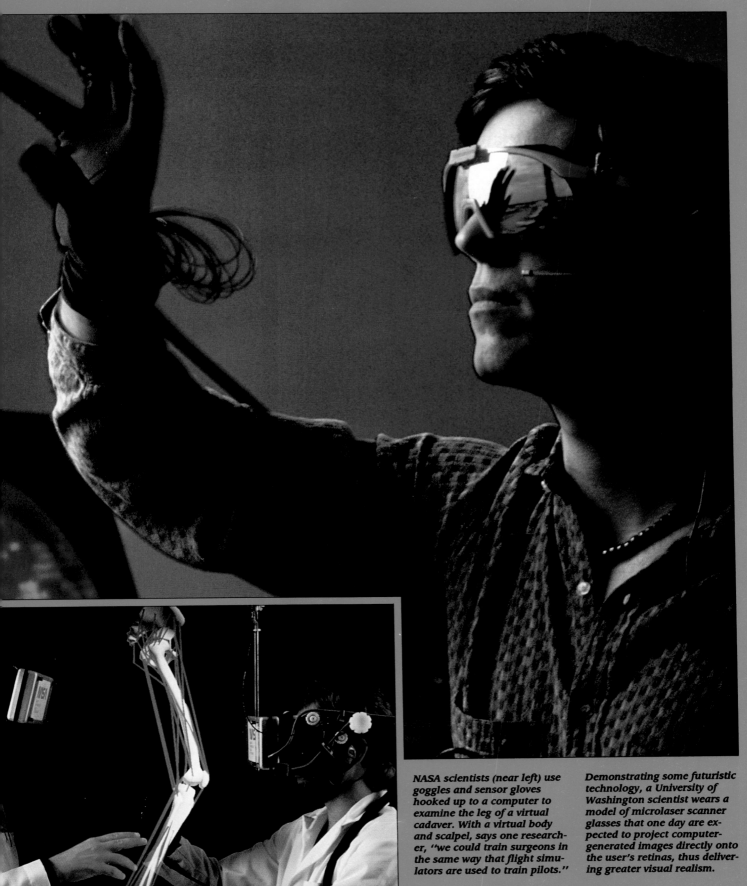

NASA scientists (near left) use goggles and sensor gloves hooked up to a computer to examine the leg of a virtual cadaver. With a virtual body and scalpel, says one researcher, "we could train surgeons in the same way that flight simulators are used to train pilots."

Demonstrating some futuristic technology, a University of Washington scientist wears a model of microlaser scanner glasses that one day are expected to project computer-generated images directly onto the user's retinas, thus delivering greater visual realism.

Pedaling through an imaginary countryside holds an added surprise for the virtual cyclist above—at a speed of twenty-five miles per hour, her bicycle will appear to leave the ground. "It was wonderful," enthused one rider of the flying bike. "I didn't want to take off the mask."

A video-arcade driving simulator with a "force feedback" steering wheel makes the ride so convincing that some drivers come prepared with motion-sickness medicine.

The Ultimate Video Game

Nearly any feat imaginable is possible in the virtual universe—swimming to the bottom of the ocean, riding a camel through the eye of a needle, leaping tall buildings at a single bound. With such adventures a mere computer chip away, many people see entertainment as the most obvious application for the new technology. Yet not all such uses are trivial amusements. With a tele-

phone hookup, for example, an absent father could play catch with his children in a virtual ballpark. And virtual technology makes games and sports accessible to the physically disabled as never before. "Right now," says one scientist, "we can build virtual worlds for quadriplegics in which they can move and behave just as well as if they weren't handicapped."

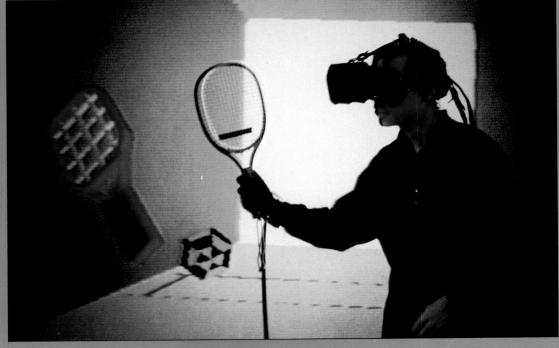

Virtual sports enthusiast Chris Allis swings his racquet in anticipation of a racquetball game with a wheelchair-bound opponent. Although Allis runs, jumps, and dives for the ball as if playing a normal match, his opponent can easily keep up using simple hand movements.

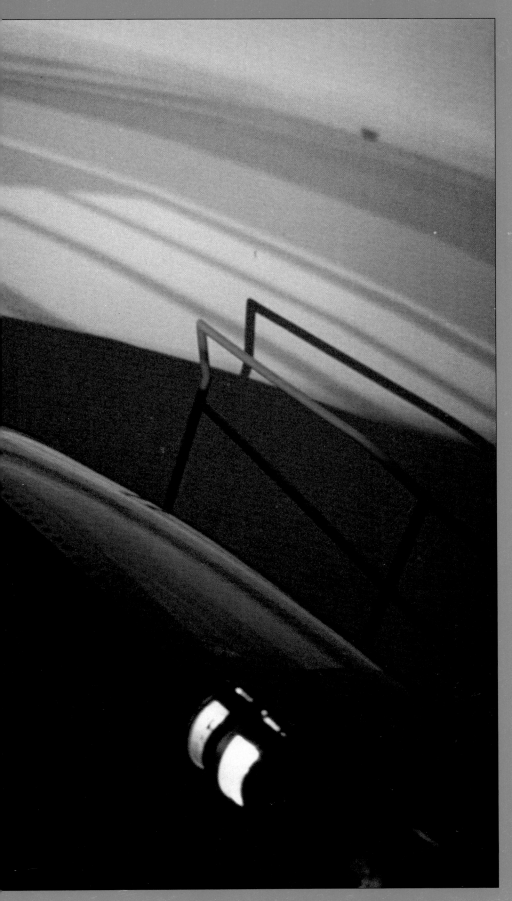

In the cockpit of an F-111 fighter-jet simulator, an air force pilot "comes in for a landing" on a highly realistic, computer-generated airstrip. The image—richer in detail, sharpness, and color than the usual virtual-reality projection—is achieved through the use of a far more powerful computer than those employed in most systems.

An Infinity of Adventures to Come

"With the technology of virtual reality," declares Thomas Furness, director of Seattle's Human Interface Technology Laboratory, "we can change the world." Proponents of the phenomenon envision people going to work in virtual office buildings, traveling to virtual vacation resorts, and shopping at virtual malls—all without leaving home. The influence of virtual reality is expected to extend to other worlds as well. With data collected by unmanned NASA spacecraft, says research scientist Michael McGreevy, "we will be able to re-create the surface of Venus in virtual reality and explore it almost as you would your office."

Jaron Lanier views the technology's power in more personal terms. Babies, he says, have "an astonishing liquid infinity of imagination" that is thwarted by the resistance of the physical world—"a fundamental indignity." Virtual reality "doesn't resist us." It restores the infinite possibilities. "That's why virtual reality electrifies people," he says. "In the future I see it as a medium of communications where people improvise worlds instead of words, making up dreams to share."

ACKNOWLEDGMENTS

The editors wish to thank the following individuals and institutions for their valuable assistance in the preparation of this volume:

Patricia H. Allderidge, The Bethlem Royal Hospital Archives and Museum, Beckenham, Kent, England; François Avril, Conservateur, Département des Manuscrits, Bibliothèque Nationale, Paris; Joseph Carey, Society for Neuroscience, Washington, D.C.; Dr. Johann Feilacher, Haus der Künstler, Niederösterreichisches Landeskrankenhaus, Klosterneuberg, Austria; Dr. Thomas Furness, University of Washington, Seattle; David Goldblatt, Littleton, New Hampshire; Dr. John R. Hughes, University of Illinois Medical Center, Chicago; Bob Jacobson, University of Washington, Seattle; Professor Daniel Keyes, Ohio University, Athens; Myron Krueger, Vernon, Connecticut; Professor Luis Eduardo Luna, Swedish School of Economics, Helsinki, Finland; Dr. Peter Michel, Aquamarin Verlag, Grafing, Germany; Renato Minozzi, Centro di Telsen-Sao, Portogruaro, Rome; Laura del Pra, Centro di Telsen-Sao, Portogruaro, Rome; Dr. Richard Restak, Washington, D.C.; Dr. Johanna Senigl, Internationale Stiftung Mozarteum, Salzburg, Austria.

BIBLIOGRAPHY

Alexander, Franz G., *The History of Psychiatry.* New York: Harper & Row, 1966.

Bailey, Ronald H., *The Role of the Brain* (Human Behavior series). New York: Time-Life Books, 1975.

Barrett, William, *Death of the Soul: From Descartes to the Computer.* Garden City, N.Y.: Doubleday, 1986.

Benson, Herbert, and William Proctor, *Your Maximum Mind.* New York: Times Books, 1987.

Bermar, Amy, "Myron Krueger." *Network World,* February 4, 1991.

Blakemore, Colin, *Mechanics of the Mind.* Cambridge, England: Cambridge University Press, 1977.

Blakemore, Colin, and Susan Greenfield, eds., *Mindwaves: Thoughts on Intelligence, Identity and Consciousness.* New York: Basil Blackwell, 1987.

Blakeslee, Thomas R., *The Right Brain.* Garden City, N.Y.: Doubleday, 1980.

Bloom, Floyd E., and Arlyne Lazerson, *Brain, Mind, and Behavior.* New York: W. H. Freeman, 1988.

Borges, Jorge Luis. *The Aleph and Other Stories.* Transl. by Norman Thomas di Giovanni. New York: E. P. Dutton, 1970.

Bowers, Barbara, *What Color Is Your Aura?* New York: Pocket Books, 1989.

Brackman, Arnold C., *A Delicate Arrangement: The Strange Case of Charles Darwin and Alfred Russel Wallace.* New York: Times Books, 1980.

Brownlee, Shannon, "A Riddle Wrapped in a Mystery." *Discover,* October 1985.

Capra, Fritjof, *The Tao of Physics.* Toronto: Bantam Books, 1988.

Cardinal, Roger, *Outsider Art.* London: Studio Vista, 1972.

Castle, Kit, and Stefan Bechtel, *Katherine, It's Time: An Incredible Journey into the World of a Multiple Personality.* New York: Harper & Row, 1989.

Chance, Paul, "The Divided Self." *Psychology Today,* September 1986.

Chase, Truddi, *When Rabbit Howls: The Troops for Truddi Chase.* New York: Jove, 1990.

Cohen, Scott, *Creativity: What Is It?* New York: M. Evans, 1977.

Copony, Heita, *Mystery of Mandalas.* Wheaton, Ill.: Theosophical Publishing House, 1989.

Cousins, Norman:
Head First: The Biology of Hope. New York: E. P. Dutton, 1989.
"Proving the Power of Laughter." *Psychology Today,* October 1989.

Ditlea, Steve, "Grand Illusion." *New York,* August 6, 1990.

Druckman, Daniel, and John A. Swets, eds., *Enhancing Human Performance.* Washington, D.C.: National Academy Press, 1988.

Drury, Nevill, *The Elements of Human Potential.* Longmead, Dorset, England: Element Books, 1989.

Editors of Prevention Magazine Health Books, *Maximum Brainpower.* Emmaus, Penn.: Rodale Press, 1989.

Editors of Time-Life Books:
Cosmos (Voyage through the Universe series). Alexandria, Va.: Time-Life Books, 1989.
Mysteries of the Human Body (Library of Curious and Unusual Facts). Alexandria, Va.: Time-Life Books, 1990.
Psychic Voyages (Mysteries of the Unknown series). Alexandria, Va.: Time-Life Books, 1987.

Elvee, Richard Q., ed., *Mind in Nature.* San Francisco: Harper & Row, 1982.

Eros + Cosmos in Mandala (exhibition catalog). Tokyo: Seibu Museum of Art.

European Outsiders (exhibition catalog). Vienna, Austria: The Gérard A. Schreiner and John L. Notter Collection, 1986.

Evans, Hilary, *Alternate States of Consciousness: Unself, Otherself, and Superself.* Wellingborough, Northamptonshire, England: Aquarian Press, 1989.

Fackelmann, K. A., "Interviews Unmask Multiple Personalities." *Science News,* May 19, 1990.

Ferguson, Marilyn, *The Brain Revolution.* New York: Taplinger, 1973.

Friedman, Joe, "Freud's Guilty Secret." *The Unexplained* (London), Vol. 13, Issue 148.

Gaffney, Tim, "Tool Puts Mind over Matter." *Dayton Daily News,* June 24, 1991.

Gardner, R. Allen, Beatrix T. Gardner, and Thomas E. Van Cantfort, eds., *Teaching Sign Language to Chimpanzees.* Albany: State University of New York Press, 1990.

Gaunt, William, *Painters of Fantasy.* Oxford, England: Phaidon Press, 1985.

Gawain, Shakti, *Creative Visualization.* San Rafael, Calif.: New World Library, 1978.

Gawain, Shakti, and Laurel King, *Living in the Light.* San Rafael, Calif.: New World Library, 1986.

Gazzaniga, Michael S., "The Split Brain in Man." *Scientific American,* August 1967.

Gorney, Cynthia:
"One Woman Becomes 6 Witnesses at Rape Trial." *Washington Post,* November 8, 1990.
"Voices from a Fractured Past." *Washington Post,* November 10, 1990.

Goswamy, B. N., *Essence of Indian Art* (exhibition catalog). San Francisco: Asian Art Museum of San Francisco, 1986.

Graef, Hilda, *The Story of Mysticism.* Garden City, N.Y.: Doubleday, 1965.

Gregory, Richard, ed., *The Oxford Companion to the Mind.* Oxford: Oxford University Press, 1987.

Hamblin, Dora Jane, "Idiot Savants." *Life,* March 18, 1966.

Hayward, Jeremy W., *Perceiving Ordinary Magic: Science and Intuitive Wisdom.* Boston: New Science Library, 1984.

Herbert, W., "The Three Brains of Eve: EEG Data." *Science News,* May 29, 1982.

Hooper, Judith, and Dick Teresi, *The Three-Pound Universe.* New York: Dell, 1986.

Howe, Michael J. A., *Fragments of Genius: The Strange Feats of Idiots Savants.* London: Routledge, 1989.

Hughes, John R., et al., "Brain Mapping in a Case of Multiple Personality." *Clinical Electroencephalography,* Vol. 21, No. 4, 1990.

Huxley, Aldous, *Collected Essays.* New York: Harper & Brothers, 1923.

Into the Unknown. Pleasantville, N.Y.: Reader's Digest Association, 1981.

"Jaron Lanier." *Omni,* January 1991.

Jastrow, Robert, *The Enchanted Loom: Mind in the Universe.* New York: Simon and Schuster, 1981.

Jaynes, Julian, *The Origins of Consciousness in the Breakdown of the Bicameral Mind.* Boston: Houghton Mifflin, 1976.

Johnson, Robert, "Outer-Space Tunes Make Earth Debut in a Bar in Peoria." *The Wall Street Journal,* September 4, 1990.

Jung, Carl G., *Mandala Symbolism.* Transl. by R. F. C. Hull. Princeton, N.J.: Princeton University Press, 1972.

Jung, Carl G., et al., *Man and His Symbols.* Garden City, N.Y.: Doubleday, 1964.

Kenny, Michael G., *The Passion of Ansel Bourne.* Washington, D.C.: Smithsonian Institution Press, 1986.

Keyes, Daniel, *The Minds of Billy Milligan.* New York: Random House, 1981.

Kingston, Jeremy, *Healing without Medicine.* Garden City, N.Y.: Doubleday, 1976.

Klein, H. Arthur, *Graphic Worlds of Peter Bruegel the Elder.* New York: Dover, 1963.

Klingender, F. D., *Goya.* London: Sidgwick and Jackson, 1948.

Laing, R. D.:
The Politics of Experience. New York: Random House, 1967.
Wisdom, Madness and Folly: The Making of a Psychiatrist. New York: McGraw-Hill, 1985.

Leary, Timothy, *Flashbacks.* Los Angeles: J. P. Tarcher, 1983.

LeShan, Lawrence, *The Medium, the Mystic, and the Physicist: Toward a General Theory of the Paranormal.* New York: Viking Press, 1974.

Levy, Steven, "Brave New Worlds." *Rolling Stone,* June 14, 1990.

Lilly, John C., *The Center of the Cyclone: An Autobiography of Inner Space.* New York: Julian Press, 1985.

Ludtke, Melissa, "Can the Mind Help Cure Disease?" *Time,* March 12, 1990.

Luna, Luis Eduardo, "The Ayahuasca Visions of Pablo Amaringo." *Shaman's Drum,* summer 1990.

Luria, A. R., *The Mind of a Mnemonist.* Transl. by Lynn Solotaroff. Cambridge, Mass.: Harvard University Press, 1968.

MacGregor, John M., *The Discovery of the Art of the Insane.*

Princeton, N.J.: Princeton University Press, 1989.

Madigan, Carol Orsag, and Ann Elwood, *Brainstorms & Thunderbolts*. New York: Macmillan, 1983.

"Maharishi's Solution to International Conflicts Confirmed Again during Assembly." *MIU World* (Fairfield, Iowa), Vol. 1, No. 1.

Maranto, Gina, "The Mind within the Brain." *Discover,* May 1984.

Maxwell, Jessica, "Fantasia." *Omni,* June 1988.

"Mind over Matter." *Discover,* August 1990.

Mookerjee, Ajit, *Kundalini: The Arousal of the Inner Energy.* London: Thames and Hudson, 1989.

Moravec, Hans, *Mind Children: The Future of Robot and Human Intelligence.* Cambridge, Mass.: Harvard University Press, 1988.

Murray, David J., *A History of Western Psychology.* Englewood Cliffs, N.J.: Prentice-Hall, 1983.

Mysteries of the Unexplained. Pleasantville, N.Y.: Reader's Digest Association, 1982.

Navratil, Leo, "Art: Bridge between Normality and Psychosis." *DU,* September 1979.

"Norman Cousins Helps Other Patients As He Once Helped Himself—By Laughing." *Good Housekeeping,* November 1989.

Ostrander, Sheila, and Lynn Schroeder, with Nancy Ostrander, *Superlearning.* New York: Dell, 1979.

Ostrom, Joseph, *You and Your Aura.* Wellingborough, Northamptonshire, England: 1987.

Peale, Norman Vincent, *The Power of Positive Living.* New York: Doubleday, 1990.

Pearce, Joseph Chilton, *The Crack in the Cosmic Egg.* New York: Crown, 1988.

Pelletier, Kenneth R., *Toward a Science of Consciousness.* Berkeley, Calif.: Celestial Arts, 1978.

Penfield, Wilder:
The Mystery of the Mind. Princeton, N.J.: Princeton University Press, 1975.
No Man Alone: A Neurosurgeon's Life. Boston: Little, Brown, 1977.

Perrott, Roy, "The Man Who Says We're All Mad." *The Observer,* September 20, 1970.

Peterson, Ivars, "Combining a Person's Live Video Image with Computer Graphics Suggests Novel Ways of Working and Playing with Computers." *Science News,* June 22, 1985.

"Psychic Research: LSD—And All That." *Time,* March 29, 1963.

Rapoport, Judith, *The Boy Who Couldn't Stop Washing.* New York: E. P. Dutton, 1989.

"R. D. Laing." *Omni,* April 1988.

Ree, Jonathan, *Descartes.* New York: Pica Press, 1974.

Reed, Graham, *The Psychology of Anomalous Experience.* Buffalo: Prometheus Books, 1988.

Restak, Richard M.:
The Brain. Toronto: Bantam Books, 1984.
The Mind. Toronto: Bantam Books, 1988.

Rogo, D. Scott, *The Infinite Boundary.* New York: Dodd, Mead, 1987.

Roy, Archie:
"The Genius Within." *The Unexplained* (London), Vol. 11, Issue 126.
"Squatters in the Mind." *The Unexplained* (London), Vol. 10, Issue 119.

Sacks, Oliver, *The Man Who Mistook His Wife for a Hat.* New York: Harper & Row, 1987.

Sagan, Carl, *Broca's Brain.* New York: Random House, 1979.

Samuels, Mike, and Nancy Samuels, *Seeing with the Mind's Eye.* New York: Random House, 1975.

Schreiber, Flora Rheta, *Sybil.* Chicago: Henry Regnery, 1973.

Schul, Bill, *The Psychic Frontiers of Medicine.* New York: Fawcett, 1977.

Shelley, Mary, *Frankenstein, or, The Modern Prometheus.* Berkeley, Calif.: University of California Press, 1984.

Shepard, Leslie A., ed., *Encyclopedia of Occultism and Parapsychology.* Detroit: Gale Research, 1984.

Shone, Ronald, *Creative Visualization: How to Use Imagery and Imagination for Self-Improvement.* Rochester, Vt.: Destiny Books, 1988.

Sizemore, Chris Costner, *A Mind of My Own.* New York: William Morrow, 1989.

Smith, Anthony, *The Mind.* New York: Viking Press, 1984.

Sonneastro: Die Künstler aus Gugging (exhibition catalog). Vienna, Austria: Kulturabteilung und das Haus der Künstler in Gugging, 1990.

Stewart, Doug, "Through the Looking Glass into an Artificial World—Via Computer." *Smithsonian,* January 1991.

Stipp, David, "Does That Computer Have Something on Its Mind?" *The Wall Street Journal,* March 19, 1991.

Storr, Anthony, *Churchill's Black Dog, Kafka's Mice, and Other Phenomena of the Human Mind.* New York: Grove Press, 1988.

"Sun Myung Moon." *Time,* July 12, 1982.

Tansley, David V., *Subtle Body: Essence and Shadow.* New York: Thames and Hudson, 1988.

Taubes, Gary:
"Einstein's Dream." *Discover,* December 1983.
"Everything's Now Tied to Strings." *Discover,* November 1986.

Taylor, Eugene, *William James on Exceptional Mental States.* New York: Scribners, 1982.

Taylor, Gordon Rattray, *The Natural History of the Mind.* New York: E. P. Dutton, 1979.

Terrace, H. S., "How Nim Chimpsky Changed My Mind." *Psychology Today,* November 1979.

"This Is Tania." *Time,* June 3, 1974.

Treffert, Darold A., *Extraordinary People: Understanding Savant Syndrome.* New York: Ballantine Books, 1989.

"Voices from a Fractured Past." *Washington Post,* November 10, 1990.

Waldrop, M. Mitchell, *Man-Made Minds: The Promise of Artificial Intelligence.* Walker, 1987.

Wehr, Gerhard, *An Illustrated Biography of C. G. Jung.* Transl. by Michael H. Kohn. Boston: Shambhala, 1989.

Weil, Andrew, *The Natural Mind.* Boston: Houghton Mifflin, 1986.

"Why People Join." *Time,* December 4, 1978.

Wilbur, Ken, ed., *The Holographic Paradigm and Other Paradoxes.* Boston: New Science Library, 1985.

Wilson, Colin, *Mysteries.* New York: Pedigree Books, 1978.

Wing-Tsit Chan, *A Source Book in Chinese Philosophy.* Princeton, N.J.: Princeton University Press, 1963.

Yates, Frances A., *The Art of Memory.* Chicago: University of Chicago Press, 1966.

Yatri, *Unknown Man* (photographs). New York: Simon & Schuster, 1988.

Yeaple, Frank, "Live Video and Animated Graphics Are Interfaced Effortlessly." *Design News,* August 18, 1986.

Young, Patrick, *Schizophrenia.* New York: Chelsea House, 1988.

Yule, John-David, ed., *Concise Encyclopedia of the Sciences.* New York: Nostrand Reinhold, 1978.

Zukav, Gary, *The Dancing Wu Li Masters.* New York: William Morrow, 1979.

PICTURE CREDITS

The sources for the pictures are given below. Credits from left to right are separated by semicolons, from top to bottom by dashes.

Cover: Art by Stansbury, Ronsaville, Wood, Inc., copied by Larry Sherer. 6, 7: Art by Stansbury, Ronsaville, Wood, Inc. 9: From *Das Mysterium des Mandalas* by Heita Copony, Aquamarin Verlag, Grafing, Germany, 1988. 11: Archives Tallandier, Paris. 12: Photo by Lennart Nilsson, *Behold Man*, Little, Brown, 1978—Jean-Loup Charmet, Paris. 14: Oeffentliche Kunstsammlung Basel Kunstmuseum. 15: Foto Claus Hansmann, Munich—from *Kundalini: The Arousal of the Inner Energy* by Ajit Mookerjee, Thames and Hudson, London, 1989. 16: Foto Claus Hansmann, Munich. 18, 19: Archiv für Kunst und Geschichte, Berlin. 21: Mary Evans Picture Library, London; The Granger Collection, New York. 22: Mary Evans Picture Library, London/Sigmund Freud Copyright. 23: The Granger Collection, New York; Erbengemeinschaft C. G. Jung, Baden, Switzerland. 24: Ann Ronan Picture Library, Taunton, Somerset. 26: Courtesy of Penfield Archives, Montreal Neurological Institute—from *Something Hidden: A Biography of Wilder Penfield* by Jefferson Lewis, Doubleday, New York, 1981. 27: © Dirk Bakker, Huntington Woods, Michigan. 29: Art by Stansbury, Ronsaville, Wood, Inc. 30: Art by Time-Life Books—photo by Jackie Earnest, courtesy Barbara Bowers, Del Mar, California. 31-33: Art by Time-Life Books. 34, 35: Art by Stansbury, Ronsaville, Wood, Inc., based on visions and drawings by Barbara Bowers, silhouettes by Time-Life Books. 36, 37: Questionnaire from the book *What Color Is Your Aura?* by Barbara Bowers, published by Pocket Books, a division of Simon & Schuster, © 1989 by Barbara Bowers. 39: From *Das Mysterium des Mandalas* by Heita Copony, Aquamarin Verlag, Grafing, Germany, 1988. 40, 41: Ann Ronan Picture Library, Taunton, Somerset. 42, 43: H. S. Terrace, Columbia University (3); Enrico Ferorelli, New York—Sue Savage-Rumbaugh/GSU/Yerkes Primate Center. 44: From *Neuropsychologia,* Vol. 9, Pergamon Press, Elmsford, New York, 1971. 46: Foto Claus Hansmann, Munich. 48: Angelo M. Caggiano/Rodale Stock Images, Emmaus, Pennsylvania. 49: The Granger Collection, New York. 50: Jean-Loup Charmet, Paris. 51: Ann Ronan Picture Library, Taunton, Somerset (6)—Danuta Otfinowski/Dot Pictures, New York. 54, 55: Index Stock/Black Box, New York. 57: The Granger Collection, New York. 58, 59: From *Congestorium Artificiose Memoria* by Johannes Host de Romberch, Venice, 1533. 60: Bill Eppridge for *Life.* 61: From *Nadia: A Case of Extraordinary Drawing Ability in an Autistic Child* by Lorna Selfe, Academic Press, London, 1977. 63: © Johann Feilacher, Haus der Künstler, Klosterneuburg, Austria (detail from page 65). 64, 65: Michael

Wolf/Visum, Hamburg; © Johann Feilacher, Haus der Künstler, Klosterneuburg, Austria (2). 66-69: © Johann Feilacher, Haus der Künstler, Klosterneuburg, Austria. 71: From *Das Mysterium des Mandalas* by Heita Copony, Aquamarin Verlag, Grafing, Germany, 1988. 72: Guttmann-Maclay Collection, Bethlem Hospital Museum, Beckenham, Kent. 73: Biblioteca Nacional, Madrid, from *Goya: In the Democratic Tradition* by F. D. Klingender, Sidgwick and Jackson, London, 1948. 74: Ann Ronan Picture Library, Taunton, Somerset. 75: Foto Claus Hansmann, Munich; Mary Evans Picture Library, London. 76: David Goldblatt, Littleton, New Hampshire—Camera Press, London. 77: David Goldblatt, Littleton, New Hampshire—Tony Buczko, Burch House. 80: Culver Pictures, Inc. 81: John R. Hughes, M.D., Ph.D., Department of Neurology, University of Illinois Medical Center at Chicago (2)—from *When Rabbit Howls* by Truddi Chase, Berkley/Jove, New York, 1990. 83: Courtesy Cornelia B. Wilbur, M.D., Lexington, Kentucky. 84, 85: Daniel Keyes—art by Billy Milligan, photographed by Daniel Keyes (6). 86: Courtesy Kit Castle; drawing by Kit Castle. 88: National Portrait Gallery, London—wood engraving by Barry Moser, from *Frankenstein* by Mary Shelley, © 1984 Pennyroyal Press. 89: Derek Bayes/Aspect Picture Library, London; Salzburger Museum Carolino Augusteum, Salzburg. 91: Giraudon, Paris. 93: Wade Davis (detail from page 95). 94, 95: The Bettmann Archive, New York; Wade Davis; Archiv für Kunst und Geschichte, Berlin. 96, 97: Herbert Benson, M.D., Harvard Medical School, New England Deaconess Hospital, Boston; Süddeutscher Verlag Bilderdienst, Munich (2). 98, 99: Archives Tallandier, Paris; The Bettmann Archive, New York; Kim Chon Kil/Gamma Liaison, New York (2)—Süddeutscher Verlag Bilderdienst, Munich. 101: From *Das Mysterium des Mandalas* by Heita Copony, Aquamarin Verlag, Grafing, Germany, 1988. 102, 103: The Bettmann Archive, New York. 105: Mary Evans Picture Library, London. 108, 109: Timothy Plowman—Pablo Amaringo, USKO-AYAR, Amazonian School of Painting, Pucallpa, Peru (2). 110, 111: Pablo Amaringo, USKO-AYAR, Amazonian School of Painting, Pucallpa, Peru. 112: Culver Pictures, Inc. 113: Wade Davis. 114, 115: From *Man and His Symbols* by Carl G. Jung et al., Doubleday, Garden City, New York, 1964; FPG, New York. 116: John Bryson. 118-121: Sergio Stingo, Naples. 123: FPG, New York. 124: Mary Evans Picture Library, London; Ron Galella Ltd., Yonkers, New York—New World Library, San Rafael, California; Steve Schapiro/Sygma, New York. 126, 127: Background photo Science Photo Library/Photo Researchers, Inc., New York—Joe Towers/Arms Communications, Woodbridge, Virginia. 129: © 1991 Peter Menzel, Napa, California (detail from page 133). 130-137: © Peter Menzel, Napa, California.

INDEX

Time-Life Books is a division of Time Life Inc.,
a wholly owned subsidiary of
THE TIME INC. BOOK COMPANY

TIME-LIFE BOOKS

Managing Editor: Thomas H. Flaherty
Director of Editorial Resources: Elise D. Ritter-Clough
Director of Photography and Research: John Conrad Weiser
Editorial Board: Dale M. Brown, Roberta Conlan, Laura
Foreman, Lee Hassig, Jim Hicks, Blaine Marshall, Rita
Thievon Mullin, Henry Woodhead

PUBLISHER: Joseph J. Ward

Associate Publisher: Ann M. Mirabito
Editorial Director: Russell B. Adams, Jr.
Marketing Director: Anne Everhart
Director of Design: Louis Klein
Production Manager: Prudence G. Harris
Supervisor of Quality Control: James King

Editorial Operations
Production: Celia Beattie
Library: Louise D. Forstall
Computer Composition: Deborah G. Tait (Manager),
Monika D. Thayer, Janet Barnes Syring, Lillian Daniels

© 1991 Time-Life Books. All rights reserved.
No part of this book may be reproduced in any form or by
any electronic or mechanical means, including informa-
tion storage and retrieval devices or systems, without
prior written permission from the publisher, except that
brief passages may be quoted for reviews.
First printing. Printed in U.S.A.
Published simultaneously in Canada.
School and library distribution by Silver Burdett Company,
Morristown, New Jersey 07960.

TIME-LIFE is a trademark of Time Warner Inc. U.S.A.

Library of Congress Cataloging in Publication Data
The Mind and Beyond / by the editors of Time-Life Books.
    p. cm.—(Mysteries of the unknown)
Includes bibliographical references and index.
ISBN 0-8094-6525-6   ISBN 0-8094-6526-4 (library)
1. Mind and body. 2. Dualism. 3. Brain. 4. Conscious-
ness. 5. Self.
I. Time-Life Books.   II. Series.
BF161.M54 1991
128'.2—dc20   91-81479
                                        CIP

MYSTERIES OF THE UNKNOWN

SERIES EDITOR: Jim Hicks
Series Administrator: Jane A. Martin
Art Director: Tom Huestis
Picture Editor: Paula York-Soderlund

Editorial Staff for *The Mind and Beyond*
Text Editors: Janet Cave (principal), Robert A. Doyle
Senior Writer: Esther R. Ferington
Associate Editors/Research: Patti H. Cass, Christian D. Kin-
ney, Sharon Obermiller
Assistant Editor/Research: Denise Dersin
Assistant Art Director: Susan M. Gibas
Writers: Marfé Ferguson Delano, Sarah D. Ince
Senior Copy Coordinator: Colette Stockum
Copy Coordinator: Donna Carey
Picture Coordinator: Betty H. Weatherley
Editorial Assistant: Donna Fountain

Special Contributors: Jennifer Mendelsohn (lead research);
Ann Louise Gates, Sheila M. Green, Patricia A. Paterno,
Evelyn S. Prettyman, Nancy J. Seeger, Priscilla Tucker
(research); John Clausen, Margery A. duMond, Donald
Jackson, Alison Kahn, Harvey S. Loomis, Gina Maranto,
Susan Perry, Peter Pocock, Daniel Stashower (text); Sara
Schneidman (consultant); John Drummond (design); Hazel
Blumberg-McKee (index).

Correspondents: Elisabeth Kraemer-Singh (Bonn), Christine
Hinze (London), Christina Lieberman (New York), Maria
Vincenza Aloisi (Paris), Ann Natanson (Rome).
Valuable assistance was also provided by Li Yan (Beijing);
Otto Gobius, Robert Kroon (Geneva); Sian Stephenson
(Helsinki); Bing Wong (Hong Kong); Judy Aspinall (Lon-
don); Trini Bandrés (Madrid); Elizabeth Brown, Kathryn
White (New York); Dag Christensen (Oslo); Ann Wise,
Leonora Dodsworth (Rome); Mary Johnson (Stockholm);
Dick Berry, Mieko Ikeda (Tokyo); Traudl Lessing (Vienna).

Other Publications:
THE NEW FACE OF WAR
HOW THINGS WORK
WINGS OF WAR
CREATIVE EVERYDAY COOKING
COLLECTOR'S LIBRARY OF THE UNKNOWN
CLASSICS OF WORLD WAR II
TIME-LIFE LIBRARY OF CURIOUS AND UNUSUAL FACTS
AMERICAN COUNTRY
VOYAGE THROUGH THE UNIVERSE
THE THIRD REICH
THE TIME-LIFE GARDENER'S GUIDE
TIME FRAME
FIX IT YOURSELF
FITNESS, HEALTH & NUTRITION
SUCCESSFUL PARENTING
HEALTHY HOME COOKING
UNDERSTANDING COMPUTERS
LIBRARY OF NATIONS
THE ENCHANTED WORLD
THE KODAK LIBRARY OF CREATIVE PHOTOGRAPHY
GREAT MEALS IN MINUTES
THE CIVIL WAR
PLANET EARTH
COLLECTOR'S LIBRARY OF THE CIVIL WAR
THE EPIC OF FLIGHT
THE GOOD COOK
WORLD WAR II
HOME REPAIR AND IMPROVEMENT
THE OLD WEST

*For information on and a full description of any of the Time-
Life Books series listed above, please call 1-800-621-7026 or
write:*
Reader Information
Time-Life Customer Service
P.O. Box C-32068
Richmond, Virginia 23261-2068

This volume is one of a series that examines the history
and nature of seemingly paranormal phenomena. Other
books in the series include:

Mystic Places	*Search for the Soul*
Psychic Powers	*Transformations*
The UFO Phenomenon	*Dreams and Dreaming*
Psychic Voyages	*Witches and Witchcraft*
Phantom Encounters	*Time and Space*
Visions and Prophecies	*Magical Arts*
Mysterious Creatures	*Utopian Visions*
Mind over Matter	*Secrets of the Alchemists*
Cosmic Connections	*Eastern Mysteries*
Spirit Summonings	*Earth Energies*
Ancient Wisdom and Secret Sects	*Cosmic Duality*
Hauntings	*Mysterious Lands and*
Powers of Healing	*Peoples*